Unplugged Tots

Introduce children to the foundations of computer coding

Unplugged Tots:

Introduce children to the foundations of computer coding

by Hannah Hagon

ISBN: 978-1-916868-22-9

Copyright © 2025 Hannah Hagon

Unplugged Tots® and the Unplugged Tots logo® are registered trademarks of Unplugged Endeavours Ltd.

Printed in the United Kingdom

Published by Raspberry Pi Ltd, 194 Science Park, Cambridge, CB4 0AB

Raspberry Pi Ireland Ltd, 25 North Wall Quay, D01 H104

compliance@raspberrypi.com

Editor: Mark Frauenfelder

Copy Editor: Sarah Cunningham

Designer: Jack Willis

Illustrator: Sam Alder

Publishing Director: Brian Jepson

CEO: Eben Upton

August 2025: First Edition

Unplugged Tots

Introduce children to the foundations of computer coding

HANNAH HAGON

Contents

Acknowledgements

Unplugged Tots simply wouldn't exist if it weren't for my daughters and husband. I am so grateful to you for being my inspiration, my sounding boards, and my teachers. Thank you for the giggles, the messy mishaps, and for reminding me every day why this work matters. I love you all so much — stay awesome!

Thanks and love also go to my parents, my sister, and her family — love you always.

Huge thank-yous and acknowledgements go to Dr. Valerie Critten and Emeritus Professor David Messer, both of the Open University. I have loved working with you both on our research projects and articles.

Thank you to the CamJam community (Raspberry Pi fans in Cambridge, UK) for accepting me into the fold with my paper, pens, and cloud dough, and not a Raspberry Pi in sight! You saw children engaged and having fun exploring early coding concepts, and kept inviting me back! As you know, this led to a chat with Raspberry Pi's CEO, Eben Upton, and now here we are: *Unplugged Tots* the book, published by Raspberry Pi Press, is out in the world. The impact has been profound, and I'm forever grateful. Thank you, CamJam!

To the folks at Raspberry Pi — Eben, Brian, Sarah, Sam, and Jack — thank you for everything. It has been an absolute pleasure watching my words and ideas evolve into something truly stunning. Thank you to my editor, Mark Frauenfelder, for all your hard work refining my words and turning them into this. Your experience and guidance have helped me more than you know.

And last but not least, to the parents and grown-ups who have supported Unplugged Tots from the beginning and are now reading this: thank you. Thank you for trusting me. Thank you for welcoming me into your living rooms and classrooms so that I can help your children grow. And thank you from your children! You're giving them space to be curious, time to connect, and permission to explore; in other words, you're giving them the gift of play, possibility, freedom, and fun — and that warms my heart.

Enjoy!

Hannah Hagon

Editor's note

While many books spring from an author's intellectual curiosity, Hannah's emerged from a parent's moment of clarity — watching her young daughters struggle to interact with a supposedly child-friendly programming language. This personal experience transformed into a mission (then into a brand, and now into a book), infusing her work with a contagious passion and enthusiasm that made it a joy to edit. Though I wish Hannah's book had been available when my daughters were young, I'm keeping copies ready for when they begin teaching computational thinking to their own children one day. Some books have a way of transcending generations, and this is one of them.

Mark Frauenfelder

Foreword

The founding myth of Raspberry Pi is reasonably well known: as Director of Studies in Computer Science at St John's College, Cambridge, I sat with colleagues in 2008 wondering where all our undergraduate applicants had gone. Together, we resolved to build a cheap, programmable computer for children in an attempt to get them back. But my own journey in computing was already two decades long by that point.

Like many of my colleagues at Raspberry Pi, I am a child of the 1980s home computer revolution. My BBC Micro, with its 32K of RAM and BASIC interpreter, provided me with my first exposure to computer programming, and to engineering more broadly: the idea that a large problem could be decomposed into smaller problems; that those problems could be solved; and that the small solutions could be composed to solve the original problem. By the time I arrived at Cambridge in 1996, I'd been programming — in BASIC, assembly language, and latterly in C — for a decade.

Home computers provide a ladder which children can climb to discover an interest in, and develop an aptitude for, computer programming. And whilst enormous strides have recently been made in improving formal computing education — due in no small part to the efforts of the Raspberry Pi Foundation — informal routes remain an essential pathway into engineering subjects, particularly for students who might not consider themselves to be stereotypically academic. Here, Raspberry Pi has greatly surpassed the impact we'd hoped for, but there is always more work to do, and doing it is what gets us out of bed in the morning.

But long before I bought my own BBC Micro, and before I even typed a first tentative two-line BASIC program into the shared BBC Micro in the corner of my primary school classroom, I'd already had some experience with computer programming. Many of you will remember the series of illustrated computer books produced by Usborne in the 1980s. In one of these I found instructions for building a limerick generator: a cardboard spinner to generate random numbers, a set of lookup tables, a short program to be copied onto a long strip of paper, and a cardboard slider to mark the current position in the program. I remember offering to build copies for my classmates: "Give me a pound and I'll give you a computer!"

So, when I met Hannah at the Cambridge Raspberry Pi Jam in 2023, the idea of using offline educational activities to set the stage for future programming seemed very natural to me. As I watched my own children, Aphra and Kit, working their way through the cloud dough and colourful foam squares activities with

Hannah's girls, Charlotte and Emily, I recognised a dawning understanding of the same basic principles — sequencing, iteration, conditionals — that I had learnt from that Usborne book four decades earlier. Aphra has since graduated to educational programming environments like MatataStudio's excellent VinciBot, taking those insights with her rather than starting afresh.

Exercises like those you'll find in this book form part of a tradition that stretches even further back, past the home computer revolution, to a time when computers were so rare, and computing time so expensive, that even university students and professional engineers were encouraged to mentally simulate their programs offline before submitting them to be run as batch jobs. They remain highly relevant, even in an era of AI-assisted vibe coding, and of $4 Raspberry Pi Pico computers running high-level languages like MicroPython.

As I know from personal experience, they provide children with an even lower first rung on the ladder, reducing the conceptual leap when they encounter "real" programming environments. They provide accessible, easy-to-deploy experiences that teachers, parents, and club leaders can leverage to introduce large numbers of children to programming, without the hassle of setting up and tearing down rooms full of computers. And, perhaps most importantly, because they exist in the physical world, these experiences don't need to compete for a child's attention on a minute-by-minute basis with the myriad entertainment activities available in the virtual one.

Raspberry Pi Press provides us with new ways to pursue the Raspberry Pi mission beyond the provision of affordable hardware and software. It has been a pleasure to work with Hannah, Mark, Brian, Sarah, Sam, and Jack to make this first *Unplugged Tots* book a reality. I hope that you'll have as much fun with these activities as my family and I have, and that your children will look back on this book with the same affection that I have for the computer books of my childhood.

Eben Upton
CEO of Raspberry Pi (Trading) Ltd.
Cambridge, July 2025

1. Introduction to Unplugged Tots

What's in this chapter

The challenge
From frustration to inspiration

It started with a sprite

One sunny day in June 2018, I took my young daughters to a Raspberry Pi festival in Cambridge and watched as their eyes lit up at a colourful ScratchJr character moving across a screen. I could see they were desperate to make the sprite dance and jump themselves, to tell their own stories.

But they couldn't.

They couldn't read the instructions. They couldn't use the mouse. They couldn't understand directions or count high enough to make any of it work. All these barriers stood between my children and this magical world of coding, where they could be creators, rather than just consumers, of entertainment.

I felt frustrated — no, I felt incensed. Why should young children be deprived of learning skills that would undoubtedly be crucial to their futures? I knew I had to find a way to help them cross this divide.

What is ScratchJr?

ScratchJr is a visual coding app designed for young children. Instead of written commands, it uses colourful blocks of code that snap together like puzzle pieces, enabling children to make characters (called sprites) move and tell stories. While it's a brilliant way to introduce coding, it requires children to have already developed reading skills, mouse control, and an understanding of directions and numbers.

That's when it hit me: what if we could teach coding concepts long before children even touch a keyboard? What if we could use play and everyday objects to teach computational thinking?

I began breaking down coding into its simplest parts: algorithms, patterns, sequences, and deconstruction. What I discovered was that these key concepts didn't apply to computers alone — they were essential for solving all kinds of problems.

And that's how Unplugged Tots was born: from a mum's determination to give her children the building blocks they need to understand technology, one playful step at a time.

The solution
Teaching computational thinking through play

What do we mean by 'unplugged'? To put it simply, no electronics.

For children aged 2½ to 8 years, we don't need to use technology to teach technology. Screen-free, play-based learning works brilliantly for them, because:
- It engages all the senses — children learn by touching, moving, seeing, and doing
- It's accessible — no need for expensive equipment or storage space
- It bridges the digital divide — financial barriers to learning are reduced
- It's future-proof — while technology changes rapidly, core thinking skills remain constant

Play isn't just about entertainment; it's how children make sense of the world and their place in it. It supports their emotional, social, and physical development. Play helps children:
- Develop physical coordination
- Learn how to negotiate and collaborate with others
- Develop emotional intelligence and empathy
- Build resilience and problem-solving skills
- Discover their identity and strengths
- Exercise creativity and imagination

I've seen this first-hand. (Including one heart-stopping moment watching my seven-year-old realise she hadn't planned how to climb down from a very tall tree!)

When we guide children through unplugged activities, we're not just teaching them computational thinking skills — we're nurturing curious, confident, and capable young minds prepared to face whatever technology throws at them.

Core concepts behind Unplugged Tots

Computational thinking may sound complex, but it's built on simple ideas that young children already love to explore:

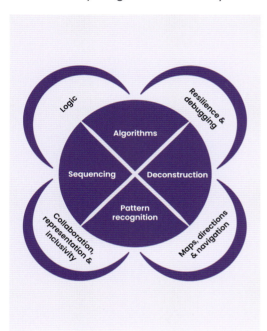

- **Deconstruction**
  (breaking big problems into smaller ones)
  Like sorting toys by type or organising a messy room

- **Pattern recognition**
  (finding things that match)
  Like creating rhythms in music or spotting repeating colours in art

- **Algorithms**
  (following sets of rules)
  Like using a recipe to make a cake or getting dressed in the morning

- **Sequencing**
  (doing things in order)
  Like safely crossing a busy road or drawing the colours of the rainbow in order

We're not teaching any new concepts here — we're giving names to things children already do and helping them apply their skills more deliberately. As children engage with these concepts, they become critical thinkers who can analyse situations from multiple angles. Their natural creativity flourishes as they discover new ways to solve problems and overcome obstacles.

Supporting skills

The four core concepts work hand in hand with four supporting skills:
- **Logic:** Asking "why?" and making sense of things
- **Debugging:** Finding and fixing mistakes
- **Navigation:** Understanding direction and space
- **Collaboration:** Working together to solve problems

The practice
Making it work in real life

Between work, cooking, endless taxi runs, and the daily hustle of keeping everything going, parents are busy. Really busy.

What we need are more adult–child learning opportunities that won't add to our already packed schedules. We're not looking to swap screen dependency for parent dependency — that wouldn't prepare our children for real life at all. Instead, we need to find ways to spend quality time together without burning ourselves out, and while continuing to encourage independent, screen-free play. We want to help our children develop naturally and keep their imaginations flowing, always using screens intentionally and only when appropriate.

This book tackles the real concerns that parents share with me every day: how to play, what to play with, and how to make these moments meaningful. It shows you how to make screen-free activities the natural, default choice rather than a constant struggle, leaving room for fun and enjoyment (for both parent and child) along the way.

Before you dive into the rest of the book, here are some useful tips to help you get the most out of the activities:

- **Each activity clearly describes everything you need,** including background context, natural conversation starters, and comic strips that make every step clear and fun to read. The best part? These activities grow right alongside your child, so you can revisit them in new ways as your little one develops.

- **Keep things simple!** We're talking 5-minute set-ups using materials you probably already have lying around. It's all about finding ways to weave learning into your daily routines. No need for fancy equipment or hours of prep — just grab what's handy and jump in. (See the FAQ on pages 6–9 for more details)

- While we're all very keen on the having fun part, **safety always comes first.** Nobody wants to fall victim to a glue-stick incident, or worse! Keep an eye on the scissors and any other dangerous equipment used, pop a newspaper down for messy play, and have wipes at the ready for moments of creative chaos. (Trust me, some of the best learning moments come with a side of mess!)

- **Your teaching style? Be yourself.** Short sessions work wonders, and following your child's curiosity is pure gold. Sprinkle in new words during play, ask questions that make them think, and remember: perfectionism has no place in playful learning.

- **You don't need any specialist knowledge** — just bring your enthusiasm and follow your child's lead. We'll be using everything from silly songs to creative crafts, turning ordinary activities into brain-boosting fun. Whether you've got 5 minutes or 50, these activities will flex to fit your family's rhythm.

Frequently asked questions (FAQ) and common concerns

I recognise that this list is not exhaustive, and that you may still have questions about how to make this work for your family. Let's tackle some of the most common concerns I hear from grown-ups:

I HATE PLAY. WILL THIS WORK FOR ME?
If you're nodding right now, you're not alone. Maybe you're unsure how to start, or worried about looking silly, or simply don't enjoy playing. That's OK. These activities aren't about forcing yourself to become a different person. They're about creating opportunities for growth and learning — sometimes through conversation rather than traditional play.

The reward? Those magical "aha!" moments when a child cracks the code of an obstacle course, beams with pride at being included in group play, or explains their morning routine with perfect logic. And yes — hearing a two-year-old pronounce 'algorithm' in their own special way never gets old!

BUT I KNOW NOTHING ABOUT TECH!
Not a problem — there's no tech involved! My focus is on computational concepts and skills, and how they can be learnt through everyday play. It's about using familiar tasks and activities as teaching opportunities.

DO I NEED TO BUY SPECIAL EQUIPMENT OR MATERIALS?
Not at all! The activities use everyday items you likely already have at home or in the classroom, and anything else can easily be found at your local craft shop or school supplies store. I've deliberately designed these activities to use readily available materials, so you can focus on the fun rather than on shopping for supplies.

WILL THESE ACTIVITIES CREATE A LOT OF MESS?

There's no glitter (I promise!) and no complicated clean-up. While we encourage creative exploration, all activities are thoughtfully designed to contain the creative chaos. I can't promise that a bit of mess won't be made from time to time, and on those occasions, newspaper sheets are your friend. Most activities use simple materials (like paper, blocks, and craft sticks) that can be quickly gathered up when you're done. The goal is to make computational thinking fun and accessible, not to create extra work for parents and teachers!

HOW LONG DOES IT TAKE TO PREPARE FOR EACH ACTIVITY?

Most activities take less than 5 minutes to set up, and many require no preparation at all. I've deliberately designed these activities to fit easily into your daily life — whether that means setting up while your bread is toasting or quickly gathering materials during naptime. The focus is on play and learning, not on elaborate preparation; even our most structured activities can be readied in moments, leaving more time for the fun part.

IS MY CHILD TOO YOUNG FOR THESE ACTIVITIES?

I conducted research with Val Critten, Doctor of Education, and David Messer, Emeritus Professor of Education (both from the Open University), demonstrating that preschool children can indeed learn programming and coding concepts through play. Published in a peer-reviewed journal, our findings show that young children learn best with adult support, and that using familiar toys leads to more success with computational activities.[1] While older children can work independently, they still enjoy shared play experiences, and maintaining an element of fun proved essential for their learning and motivation.

The research also revealed that children as young as 2½ years can grasp core computational thinking concepts, including logic, sequencing, algorithms, and debugging. The key is to use familiar toys and activities with consistent adult support. Through these experiences, children learn valuable skills such as communication and collaboration, while also developing their capacity for planning, logical thinking, and problem-solving.

---

1   Critten, V., Hagon, H., & Messer, D. (2022). 'Can Pre-school Children Learn Programming and Coding Through Guided Play Activities? A Case Study in Computational Thinking.' *Early Childhood Education Journal*, 50, 969-981.

Every child develops at their own pace, but here's a rough guide to what you might expect to see at different stages:

- **Ages 2–3:** These little explorers are just discovering structured play. Focus on the initial activity and give plenty of gentle support. Let them take the lead where possible — their natural curiosity will guide their learning more than you might expect.

- **Ages 4–5:** Time to introduce new terms to their vocabulary and encourage their leadership skills (using phrases from the comics as guidance). Start with the main activity, then try the second activity while interest is still high. If they're engaged, experiment with the debugging challenges.

- **Ages 6–8:** Ready for more complex thinking? Either jump straight into the debugging activities or build up to them gradually through the main activities, establishing core concepts and language first.

- **Ages 8+:** While originally written for younger children, these activities have captivated teenagers and adults alike. The blend of play, craft, and computational thinking transcends age — so join the fun!

WHO ARE YOU?

Hi, I'm Hannah Hagon, founder of Unplugged Tots! As a mother of two girls and former Chair of Governors at a local infant school, I've seen both sides of the educational fence. For nearly 20 years, I worked in legal tech — not as a coder, but as someone who saw how technology could transform the way we live and work.

Technology has given me countless tools that make life easier and better. But I've also seen how it can become a barrier to others, especially to young children. That's why I'm passionate about finding the right balance. I'm not a coding expert or a perfect parent (just ask my daughters!), but I am someone who believes in the power of play to teach our kids vital skills.

Like many parents, I want my children to be happy and resilient, ready for whatever their futures hold. Yes, I care about their careers — but more importantly, I want them to have the tools to think critically, solve problems creatively, and navigate an increasingly digital world with confidence.

That's really what *Unplugged Tots* is about — giving children access to these fundamental thinking skills through play, long before they need to worry about screens or keyboards. It's about creating strong foundations that will serve them well in whatever they go on to do, whether they grow up to be artists, engineers, or something we haven't even imagined yet.

Troubleshooting!

When things don't go as planned — and with young children, they often don't — there are some simple solutions you can reliably use to right some common wrongs. Remember that perfect execution isn't the goal; engagement and enjoyment are what matter most.

Problem: The child isn't engaging with the activity
- Check if they need a snack or some rest
- Switch to free play temporarily
- Start over with a simpler version, or perhaps a more advanced version
- Try again another time

Problem: The activity seems too challenging
- Return to the basic version
- Break it into smaller steps
- Reduce the complexity
- Give more direct guidance

Problem: The child wants to do something different
- Follow their lead and let them adapt the activity
- Keep using computational thinking vocabulary
- Look for more learning opportunities in their chosen direction
- Return to the original activity another day

Problem: The child struggles with the new vocabulary
- Use the new terms casually in everyday situations
- Pair new words with familiar concepts
- Model their understanding by using the words yourself
- Don't force it — let understanding develop naturally

Remember: The activities are flexible starting points. If your child takes things in an unexpected direction, that's fine — learning happens in many different ways.

Let the adventure begin!

A final word of advice before you begin: there may be times when the activities spark your child's imagination in unexpected ways, and as a mum, I say run with it! Don't feel bound by rigid instructions. If making repeating patterns with blocks leads to you building an entire LEGO® mansion together, that's wonderful; your child might encounter new problems that need debugging along the way, naturally exploring computational thinking without even realising it. What matters most is nurturing their curiosity and supporting holistic learning.

Now, let's dive in and discover lots of new words and skills together — and most importantly, go and have fun with your child!

2. Deconstruction
Breaking big problems into small parts

Activities

Essential steps

1. Select a complex task
2. Show the child how to break down the task into smaller tasks
3. Guide the child to complete each smaller task separately
4. Ask the child to break down a different problem

Success looks like

- Recognising when tasks need to be broken down
- Breaking down complex tasks into smaller parts
- Completing sub-tasks independently
- Explaining how parts make up the whole

Common challenges

- Too easy → choose more complex tasks to break down
- Too hard → start with familiar activities that have clear parts
- Child loses focus → break down fun activities, like games or stories

Introduction

Why deconstruction matters

Deconstruction is a fundamental skill that helps us tackle big challenges in manageable ways. It's the ability to break down complex problems or tasks into smaller parts, whether we're building with blocks, completing a puzzle, or following a recipe. When learning to deconstruct problems, children develop the confidence to approach seemingly overwhelming tasks. They also learn management skills that they will use in all kinds of scenarios — skills that will help them with everything from their daily routines and schoolwork to project planning and, eventually, computer programming.

Where we see deconstruction

You can find opportunities for deconstruction in everyday activities at home, at nursery, and at school. Often, it's simply about extending activities children already do, such as playing with toys, helping around the house, or participating in classroom projects. Many routine household tasks can become learning moments, and even games or activity kits can help teach these concepts. The key is to notice these natural opportunities for deconstruction and make them engaging for children.

How to explain deconstruction to children

When talking to children about deconstruction, try these kid-friendly explanations:

Adult: "We have this big problem, and to help us solve it, we need to break it down into smaller pieces — we should deconstruct it. 'Deconstruct' just means 'break it down'."

Adult: "Woah, this is a lot to think about. How can we make it easier for ourselves? Shall we break it down? Shall we deconstruct it?"

Adult: "Goodness, there's lots to do here. How about we work out what we should tackle first? Let's deconstruct our one big lots-to-do pile and turn it into lots of smaller to-do piles that we can tackle bit by bit. What do you think?"

Activity progress path

Carrying out simple sorting tasks is the first step in a child's journey towards developing sophisticated problem-solving abilities.

As children progress from basic categorisation to handling multiple variables and debugging challenges, they develop crucial physical, social, and computational thinking skills that can then be extended through additional activities.

CORE ACTIVITY: BREAKING DOWN COMPLEX TASKS

- **Basic**
  Sort items by single attributes (colour, size, type) and match simple categories
- **Intermediate**
  Organise items using multiple attributes and identify sub-tasks within larger problems
- **Advanced**
  Handle multiple variables, predict potential issues, and tackle debugging challenges

SKILLS DEVELOPMENT

- **Physical**
  Fine motor skills, spatial organisation
- **Social**
  Collaboration, communication, task sharing
- **Computational**
  Problem deconstruction, logical reasoning, sequencing, debugging

Troubleshooting tips

When helping children learn how to break down complex tasks, you may face some common challenges. Here's how to handle the situation when your child is:

- **Overwhelmed**
  Break the big task into even smaller pieces — for example, if sorting all the laundry feels too big, start by just matching socks or separating clothes by colour.
- **Frustrated**
  Watch for signs of agitation and suggest a quick movement break before it escalates. Help them see how far they've already come with the smaller parts.
- **Distracted**
  Clear the workspace and give them ownership of specific, smaller tasks; keep them engaged by celebrating each completed part before moving on to the next.
- **Rushing**
  Turn their enthusiasm into a structured challenge — "Let's tackle one small part at a time," or "Can you be the checker for this section?"
- **Losing interest**
  Make breaking down tasks playful: turn steps into a treasure hunt, competition, or story. Connect the smaller parts to things they enjoy.
- **Showing signs of perfectionism**
  Remind them that learning to break down problems involves trial and error, and share examples of times when you had to try different ways of splitting up a task.

Remember: The goal is to help children see how breaking down big tasks makes them more manageable while keeping the atmosphere light and supportive.

Get ready to break down big problems into smaller parts with **Sam** and **Emily**!

Activity
Jigsaw puzzles

Jigsaws are an excellent introduction to deconstruction. While children should have the freedom to solve puzzles in their own way, breaking down a large puzzle into manageable parts (like separating the edge pieces first) teaches them valuable problem-solving skills.

For younger children using board puzzles, focus on matching shapes and turning pieces to fit. It's up to you whether you help them from the start and if your involvement either continues to the end or tapers off — whichever way you decide is fine. For children using traditional jigsaws, try teaching them to sort the jigsaw pieces into two different piles: edge pieces and middle pieces.

Materials and prep

TIME NEEDED

- Set-up: 5 minutes
- Activity: 15–45 minutes, depending on the puzzle's complexity and the child's engagement

REQUIRED

- Age-appropriate jigsaw puzzle
- Small boxes or containers for sorting pieces
- Puzzle mat or board for if you need to pause the activity (optional)
- Clear, flat surface to work on

PREPARATION

1. Choose an appropriate difficulty level based on the child's age and experience
2. Clear a dedicated workspace
3. Check that all the puzzle pieces are present
4. Consider setting up sorting areas for edge pieces and middle pieces
5. Make sure you have the puzzle box's picture visible for reference

PUZZLING IT OUT

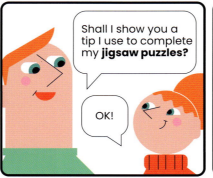

Shall I show you a tip I use to complete my **jigsaw puzzles?**

OK!

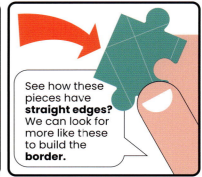

See how these pieces have **straight edges?** We can look for more like these to build the **border.**

Oh, I see! Can I find more?

Of course. Let's see how many we can find.

FOR LATER

MIDDLE

We're **deconstructing** the task by making this pile of puzzle pieces easier to work with. That's all deconstruction is — taking a big problem and breaking it down into smaller, easier-to-manage chunks.

As you're going through the edge pieces, turn them so that the pattern or image is the right way up.

To help us make this jigsaw, should we have **this side or this side facing up?**

This side!

Think about it — if we can't see the colours, how will we know what matches?

Oh, no, they have to be **this way.**

Well done, you've **debugged a problem!** Shall we connect the edge pieces now?

Let your child lead when building the border, matching colours and shapes at their own pace. Stay nearby and observe, and only step in if they show signs of frustration — this develops their independence and their observation skills.

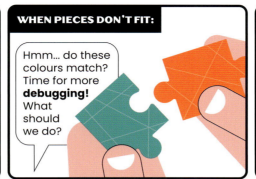

WHEN PIECES DON'T FIT:

Hmm... do these colours match? Time for more **debugging!** What should we do?

Try a **different** piece?

That's it! You're **debugging** like a pro!

When your child struggles, resist fixing the problem for them. Guide their debugging process by helping them notice mismatched colours or shapes. Return wrong pieces to the pile and encourage them to try new ones — this teaches problem-solving through trial and error. Remember to celebrate when they find the right piece.

Yay! You did it!

By staying calm and curious when facing problems, we show children that mistakes are learning opportunities, not disasters.

Complete the edge section and repeat any debugging processes you encounter.

High five! Border done! See how **deconstruction** made the puzzle easier? Ready for the middle pieces?

Sure!

Remember to look at both **colours and shapes**. Take your time — you've got this!

For the middle section, use the same approach:

Group similar colours and patterns, match shapes, and debug as needed, following the steps above where necessary. Remember to pile on that praise — your child is learning a LOT!

Congratulations!

What an amazing journey of discovery and problem-solving you've shared together!

To our Young Problem Solver: Wow, you're becoming an expert at breaking down big challenges into smaller ones! You showed amazing skill in finding edge pieces, sorting colours, and debugging to make pieces fit. You learnt that sometimes the best way to solve a big puzzle is to tackle it bit by bit. Keep using these skills whenever you face a tricky task — remember how you made the puzzle manageable by starting with the edges!

To the Adult Problem Solver: You've helped your child discover one of the most valuable skills in life — how to break down overwhelming tasks into manageable steps. Through this puzzle activity, your child has learnt about:
- Problem decomposition (breaking tasks into smaller parts)
- Systematic thinking (organising by edges, colours, patterns)
- Debugging (fixing mistakes when pieces don't match)

Keep reinforcing these deconstruction skills in your daily activities, whether you're cleaning up toys, getting ready for school, or tackling new puzzles. Remember, every time you help your child break down a big task, you're building their confidence in problem-solving. These skills will help them approach challenges throughout their life with assurance and strategy!

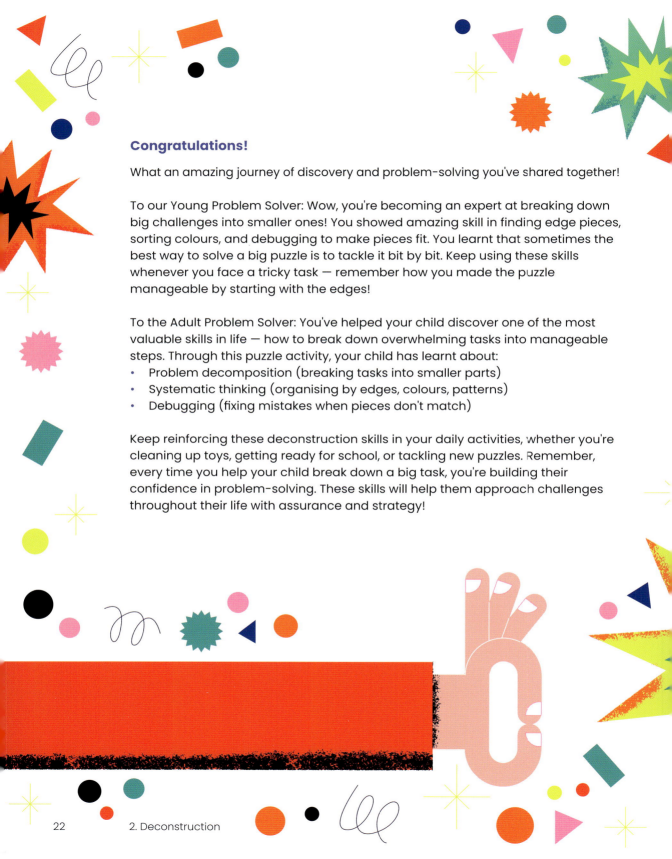

Taking it further

ADVANCING DECONSTRUCTION SKILLS

- Break larger puzzles into more sub-categories (edges, colours, patterns)
- Sort middle pieces into colour zones before assembly
- Create multiple working areas for different sections

PROBLEM-SOLVING EXTENSIONS

- Let the child create their own sorting system
- Ask the child to explain their deconstruction strategy

TEACHING OPPORTUNITIES

- Ask the child to teach someone else their method
- Compare different approaches to breaking down the task
- Challenge the child to find the fastest way to sort

Activity
Sorting the washing

Everyone has to do laundry, and when you have children, your washing machine works overtime (what's with all those socks disappearing into a portal, never to be seen again?!). While it's possibly the dullest housework activity, it's actually a perfect opportunity to teach computational thinking. By involving children in laundry sorting, we can transform this everyday task into an engaging lesson in breaking down big problems into smaller parts. Yes, it may take a little longer, but you're not just teaching common skills here — you're helping them develop problem-solving abilities that they'll use throughout their entire lives. And who knows? Maybe they'll even help solve the mystery of those vanishing socks!

Materials and prep

TIME NEEDED

- Set-up: 2 minutes
- Activity: 15–45 minutes, depending on the amount of laundry and the child's level of engagement
- Extension activities: 10–15 minutes for sock-matching game

REQUIRED

- Clean, dry washing (a mixture of easily identifiable items, including 3–4 pairs of distinctly patterned socks)
- Clear, flat surface to place clothes on
- Basket to transport the folded clothes to their final destination

PREPARATION

1. Clear a dedicated workspace to place the folded laundry on (a sofa or table works well)
2. Choose appropriate items of clothing based on the child's age, size, and experience (keep some simple items aside for confidence-building purposes)
3. Remove any complicated items that might frustrate the child
4. Set up clear zones for different family members' clothes piles

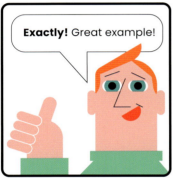

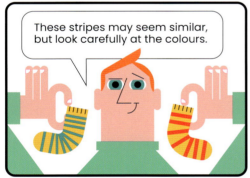

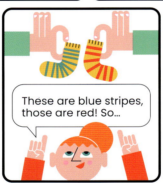

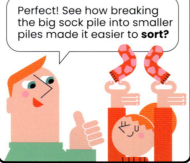

Congratulations!

Great work sorting the laundry and learning at the same time!

To our Young Sorting Champion: Woo-hoo! High five! You've done a brilliant job tackling that big pile of washing. You showed amazing skill in sorting everything into neat piles and finding matching socks. You're becoming an expert at breaking big jobs into smaller, easier ones. Plus, you've been really helpful to your family — we call that being thoughtful and kind!

To the Adult Sorting Partner: I know there will be times when you'd prefer to do this job alone and save yourself some time, but you're teaching invaluable skills here! Through this simple activity, your child has learnt how to:

- Deconstruct a big task into manageable pieces
- Problem-solve by working systematically through a jumble
- Recognise patterns (and match socks)
- Count and sort items effectively
- Exercise kindness and think about others

What might have taken you ten minutes to do alone has become a valuable learning experience between you and your child. Teaching our children these important life skills is perhaps the most rewarding part of being a parent — well, one of them... the hugs are pretty good too!

Taking it further

Games are a great way to extend a child's learning while keeping things fun and engaging. I remember doing the Robot Game with my children, and it was a hilarious activity (especially when they made me bump into the sofa!). It makes the arduous task of putting away laundry a bit more enjoyable for everyone.

NAVIGATION CHALLENGE: TURN YOUR CLOTHES DELIVERY INTO A ROBOT GAME

- Use strict forward, left, and right commands (90° angles only)
- Practise giving and following directions to each room
- Include sound effects for added entertainment

TEACHING TIPS

- Let the child lead the robot navigation
- Make deliberate 'robot errors' for debugging practice
- Celebrate successful deliveries to correct locations

Activity
Growing and debugging in the garden

Planting seeds teaches children valuable computational thinking skills through hands-on experience. Despite following all the rules, things can go wrong — from hungry squirrels and snails to temperamental weather — making this the perfect introduction to debugging.

One year, I had the idyllic notion to plant sunflowers, carrots, and marigolds with my daughters. Despite our careful watering and tending, many of the plants failed miserably! But the few successes (and even the failures) taught us important lessons about:
- Deconstruction (breaking gardening into manageable steps)
- Algorithms (following planting instructions)
- Sequencing (doing steps in the right order)
- Logic (understanding growing seasons)
- Debugging (solving problems, like pests)

Sometimes the journey matters more than the destination, and what could be better than spending some time outdoors together while learning these skills?

Materials and prep

TIME NEEDED

- Set-up: 5 minutes
- Activity: 20–45 minutes, depending on the child's engagement
- Ongoing care: a few minutes daily for watering and monitoring

GROWING EQUIPMENT

- Seeds (sunflowers work well for beginners)
- Soil or compost
- Plant pots or garden bed space
- Basic gardening tools (trowel, small spade)
- Watering can
- Plant supports (sticks and string) for later

PROTECTIVE ITEMS

- Old clothes for both the adult and the child
- Newspaper sheets or an old shower curtain for indoor workspaces
- Soap and water for clean-up

PREPARATION

1. Check the best planting times for your chosen seeds
2. Gather all your equipment
3. Have cleaning supplies at the ready
4. Create your workspace (inside or outside)

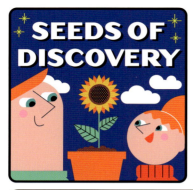

SEEDS OF DISCOVERY

Want to do some **gardening** today? We could plant some seeds and have beautiful, colourful flowers in a few months!

YEAH!

Do you remember any flowers that you like? We can learn about them together.

Sunflowers, because they're really tall.

Great choice! Sunflowers are also very clever — they follow the sun across the sky.

Wow!

What do you think we need to **grow** sunflowers?

Seeds and **soil!**

That's a great start. Let's make **a list!**

The packet tells us how to take care of our plants.

So, you already said **seeds** and **soil**. What else do we need?

Pots?

Perfect! Anything else?

Um, they get thirsty, so maybe water?

YES!

How long do you think it takes for sunflowers to grow this tall?

It would take **ages!**

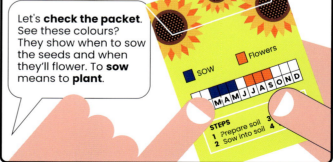

Let's **check the packet**. See these colours? They show when to sow the seeds and when they'll flower. To **sow** means to **plant**.

See this list here? These are all the steps we need to follow to grow our flowers. We can call this list an **algorithm**.

Algorithms are explored in more detail in Chapter 4.

An algorithm is a **set of rules** for us to follow.

To grow our flowers properly, we have to work **step by step.** Luckily, the packet says March is the perfect time to start!

So can we plant them now?

Almost. We should think about possible **problems** first. Like squirrels and snails — they love eating sunflowers.

OH NO!

This is where we can practise our **debugging skills.**

That's about **fixing things**, isn't it?

Exactly! **Debugging** is all about **finding and fixing errors**. Sometimes things go wrong, but that's how we learn to make things better.

But why try if things might go wrong?

Well, because we can always **prepare for problems**. For example, if the plants are too dry, what could we do?

WET THEM!

Perfect! And if they're being eaten by slugs?

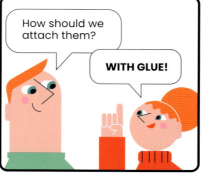

Through gardening, we have practised:

- Pattern recognition (identifying growth cycles)
- Algorithms (following planting instructions)
- Sequencing (following instructions in order)
- Debugging (solving problems)
- Working with nature
- Patience
- Asking for help

Congratulations!

You've explored the world of gardening and problem-solving together brilliantly!

To our Young Gardener: Well done for thinking about all the different steps needed to grow your sunflowers! You showed amazing thinking skills when talking about what could go wrong and how to fix problems. Keep using your problem-solving skills and wonderful imagination in everything you do.

To the Adult Gardener: Talking about the different steps in the process, as well as the rules, the equipment, and all the possible problems, helps build resilience in children. By discussing things that could go wrong before you began, you managed your child's expectations and helped them to think about solutions. Remember to encourage their imagination to keep them engaged in the activity (it's a long one!) and to build their confidence when tackling challenges.

Together, you've explored:
- Breaking down big tasks into smaller ones
- Thinking ahead about possible problems
- Using imagination to find solutions
- Building confidence through preparation
- Taking ownership of the growing process

Keep encouraging that wonderful imagination and that problem-solving spirit. Remember, sometimes the best learning happens while waiting for those seeds to grow!

Taking it further

NAVIGATION AND PLANNING

- Plan your route to the garden centre for supplies
- Choose your planting areas
- Map out where the germinated seeds will go

PATTERN WORK

- Create ABAB patterns with different flower types
- Look for natural patterns once the flowers bloom
- Sort the seeds into groups before planting

CRITICAL THINKING

- Predict what will happen when the seeds are watered
- Consider the possible outcomes of not watering the seeds
- Question if the sunlight is sufficient
- Track your daily watering schedule

TEACHING TIPS

- Guide the children to take ownership of plant care
- Encourage scientific thinking by asking them questions
  - Build understanding through 'why' questions
  - Build prediction skills through 'what if' questions

Extension ideas

If your child is enjoying learning about deconstruction, here are some ways to build on what you've already done:
* Create visual task breakdowns
* Design step-by-step guides
* Include counting and sorting challenges
* Incorporate pattern recognition tasks, games, and competitions
* Add navigation elements to the activities
* Apply deconstruction to new scenarios

Remember: These everyday activities reinforce the skills your child is already learning. They're perfect for those times when you need a quick bit of entertainment or distraction, and they build naturally on the computational thinking skills you have been practising.

Building blocks for coding in Scratch

These everyday activities build crucial pre-coding skills that will help children succeed when they come to use Scratch, such as:
* **Sorting and deconstruction**
  Just as children learn to break down puzzles into manageable parts (edges, colours, patterns) or sort laundry into smaller piles, they'll later break down coding projects into smaller sub-tasks. Experimenting with these tangible, physical activities supports children's associations and helps them process their own learning.
* **Debugging**
  The debugging process learnt through activities like puzzles (where children recognise when pieces don't fit and try new solutions) directly mirrors how they'll test and fix their Scratch code. When a project gives an unexpected result, these skills can help children break down the big problem into a series of smaller tasks.
* **Logical thinking**
  The systematic thinking used when sorting puzzle pieces, organising laundry, and planning garden layouts develops the structured approach needed at every level of computer programming, including early-age Scratch projects.

Together, these skills make the transition into learning computer sciences less daunting, giving children the confidence they need to tackle new challenges.

3. Pattern recognition
Understanding repeating elements

Activities

Essential steps

1. Create a repeating pattern using colourful blocks or other everyday items
2. Show the child how to identify the pattern
3. Ask the child to continue the pattern
4. Introduce simple pattern debugging (AB, AB, BA)

Success looks like

- Identifying repeating elements in patterns
- Continuing patterns independently
- Creating simple patterns
- Spotting pattern errors

Common challenges

- Too easy → introduce more complex pattern sequences
- Too hard → start with simple two-colour patterns
- Child loses focus → use favourite toys or objects to make patterns

Introduction

Why pattern recognition matters

Patterns can be found everywhere, in things both artificial and natural, and recognising them is a fundamental skill that helps us make sense of the world around us. Encouraging observation in children enables them to learn to identify patterns, develop the ability to predict what comes next, and solve problems more efficiently. These skills will help them in everything they go on to do, from reading, music, and artistic endeavours to mathematics and computer programming.

Where we see pattern recognition

Patterns figure constantly in our daily lives; we can help children discover them in clothing designs, on animals, in the changing seasons, in songs, and in rhythm patterns like clapping. Once children start noticing patterns in the world around them, you can explore simple AB sequences together. For example, you can support shape recognition while setting the table (fork, spoon, fork, spoon), or shape and colour recognition while sorting laundry (white sock, blue shirt, white sock, blue shirt). Using every opportunity to spot and actively seek out repeating patterns with children not only helps them later in life but is also lots of fun!

How to explain pattern recognition to children

When talking about pattern recognition with children, try these kid-friendly explanations:

> **Adult:** *"See these stripes on your top? They make a repeating pattern — green, yellow, green, yellow. We can see how the pattern carries on."*

Once the child understands simple AB patterns, you can introduce ABC patterns.

> **Adult:** *"Can you tell me what animals you see in this picture? Can you tell me the next animal in this repeating pattern sequence, please?"*

> **Adult:** *"Can you spot a repeating pattern here? It looks like there are lots of different animals, but if we look closely, we can see that the same few are actually repeating. Do you see the dog, cat, hamster, guinea pig, dog, cat, hamster, guinea pig, dog, cat, hamster, guinea pig? Can you help me spot where it starts over?"*

Activity progress path

Understanding simple patterns is the first step in a child's journey towards developing sophisticated problem-solving and logical reasoning abilities.

As children progress from spotting and creating patterns to the complex challenge of debugging repeating ones, they learn crucial physical, social, and computational thinking skills that can then be extended through additional activities.

CORE ACTIVITY: SPOTTING, CREATING, CONTINUING, AND DEBUGGING REPEATING PATTERNS

- **Basic**
  Spot and continue AB patterns using simple objects, images, shapes, and colours
- **Intermediate**
  Create ABC patterns and patterns with simple rules
- **Advanced**
  Debug incorrect patterns and design complex sequences

SKILLS DEVELOPMENT

- **Physical**
  Fine motor skills, spatial organisation, observation
- **Social**
  Collaboration, communication, task sharing
- **Computational**
  Deconstruction, problem decomposition, sequencing, logical reasoning, debugging

Troubleshooting tips

When introducing children to repeating patterns, you may face some common challenges. Here's how to handle the situation when your child is:

- **Overwhelmed**
  Break the task into shorter sessions or start with very easy repeating patterns, using familiar items or favourite colours/shapes.
- **Frustrated**
  Watch out for signs of agitation and suggest a quick break before it escalates. Moving the body helps with frustration.
- **Distracted**
  Clear the workspace and keep any other toys or activity equipment out of sight for the moment.
- **Rushing**
  Stay calm! If they're knocking objects off the surface, redirect the activity: "Oh dear, our repeating pattern isn't repeating any more, it's all mixed up. Can we work together to create a new one?"
- **Losing interest**
  Make it playful — turn repeating patterns into a colour-matching game or play spot-the-difference between the adult's and the child's patterns.
- **Showing signs of perfectionism**
  Remind them that making mistakes is part of learning — even adults get repeating patterns wrong sometimes!

Spot what comes next with
pattern detectives
Layla, **Zara**, and **Adil**!

Activity
Pattern fun with familiar objects

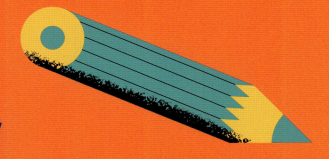

Creating patterns with familiar objects helps children feel confident and relaxed while learning. Choose matching sets of foam shapes, LEGO® or DUPLO® bricks, Mega Bloks, mini pom-poms, coloured pencils, or even different-coloured clothes pegs; clothes pegs are excellent tools for developing pincer grip, a crucial skill to have when building the muscle memory to hold pencils and eventually learn to write. Alternatively, you could use coloured pencils and plain paper to combine pattern-making with pencil grip practice. Both approaches enable children to practise patterns while learning colours and building essential motor skills.

Materials and prep

TIME NEEDED

- Set-up: 5 minutes
- Activity: 15–45 minutes, depending on the child's engagement and whether they are happy to proceed to more difficult repeating patterns

REQUIRED

- Age-appropriate objects (foam shapes, LEGO/DUPLO bricks, Mega Bloks, mini pom-poms, coloured pencils, different-coloured clothes pegs)
- Clear, flat surface to work on

PREPARATION

1. Clear a dedicated workspace
2. Remove any distractions
3. Think of an appropriate pattern based on the child's age and experience
4. Prepare your pattern objects
5. Make sure you have paper and pens handy to demonstrate pattern concepts if the child needs a visual reminder

PATTERN PLAY

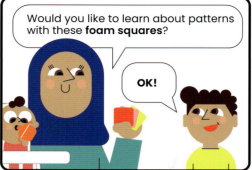

Would you like to learn about patterns with these **foam squares**?

OK!

Let's pick out the **colours** we want to use.

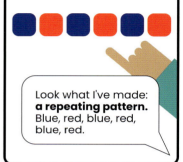

We'll sweep the rest to the side — we don't want them distracting us.

Sorting items we need and removing others helps teach deconstruction; this is explained in more detail in Chapter 2.

Look what I've made: **a repeating pattern.** Blue, red, blue, red, blue, red.

Can you point to the **first square**?

That's the **blue one!** The **next** one is...?

RED!

Great! We can find **patterns** like this everywhere, on clothes, rugs, and towels.

Want to try? Let's make another **pattern** using the blue and red squares...

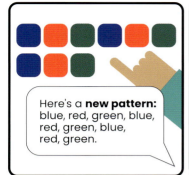

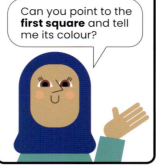

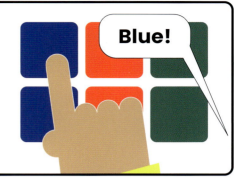

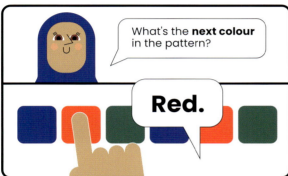

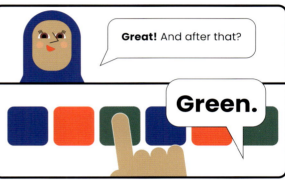

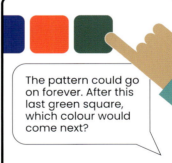

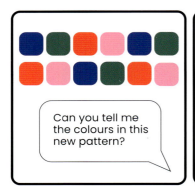

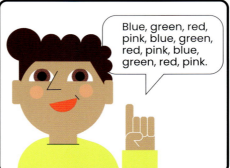

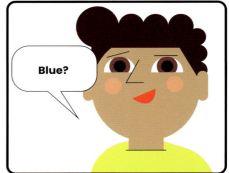

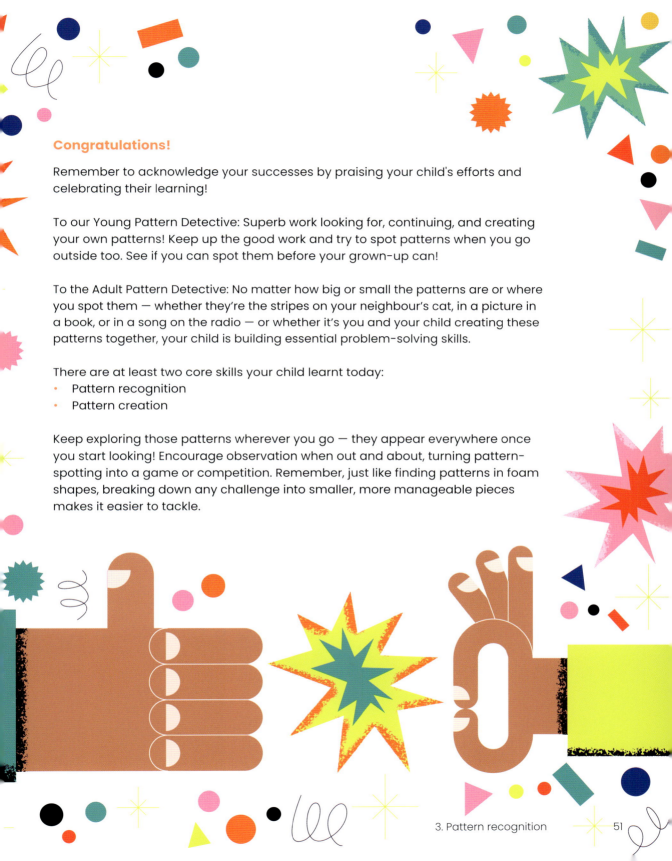

Congratulations!

Remember to acknowledge your successes by praising your child's efforts and celebrating their learning!

To our Young Pattern Detective: Superb work looking for, continuing, and creating your own patterns! Keep up the good work and try to spot patterns when you go outside too. See if you can spot them before your grown-up can!

To the Adult Pattern Detective: No matter how big or small the patterns are or where you spot them — whether they're the stripes on your neighbour's cat, in a picture in a book, or in a song on the radio — or whether it's you and your child creating these patterns together, your child is building essential problem-solving skills.

There are at least two core skills your child learnt today:
- Pattern recognition
- Pattern creation

Keep exploring those patterns wherever you go — they appear everywhere once you start looking! Encourage observation when out and about, turning pattern-spotting into a game or competition. Remember, just like finding patterns in foam shapes, breaking down any challenge into smaller, more manageable pieces makes it easier to tackle.

Taking it further

CREATIVE VARIATIONS

- Experiment with drawing different patterns on a sheet of paper: try straight lines, wavy lines, zigzags, and circles
- Make patterns with shapes (square, square, circle, circle)
- Build a story around the pattern (red blocks as houses, blue blocks as roads)
- Let the child create patterns with their chosen objects

DEBUGGING GAME

1. Create a reference pattern at the top of the workspace
2. Make an identical pattern below
3. Ask the child to identify the pattern
4. Have the child close their eyes while you rearrange the pieces
5. Ask the child to identify and then correct the new pattern

EXTENSION IDEAS

- Switch roles, letting the child create 'bugs' for you to find
- Make intentional mistakes to encourage discussion
- Use humour when identifying the wrong pieces
- Build on their success by offering new challenges

You should only introduce extensions once the basics have been mastered.

Activity
Repeating image patterns

Instead of colours or shapes, try using pictures that reflect the child's interests. This approach follows the same principles as before, but will introduce repeating patterns in a way that will stretch our children's observation skills.

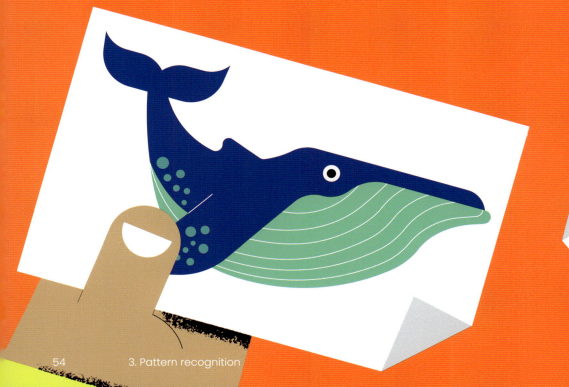

Materials and prep

TIME NEEDED

- Set-up: 5 minutes
- Activity: 15–45 minutes, depending on the child's engagement and whether they are happy to proceed to more difficult repeating patterns

REQUIRED

- Images of familiar things
- Clear, flat surface to work on

PREPARATION

1. Print or copy your chosen images and cut them out in advance
2. Clear a dedicated workspace
3. Remove any distractions
4. Have paper and pens handy to demonstrate pattern concepts if the child needs a visual reminder

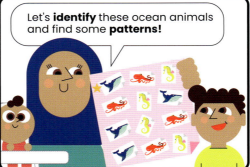

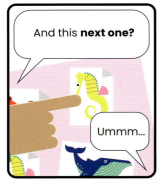

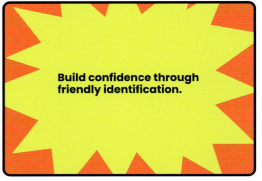

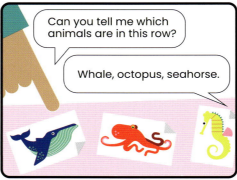

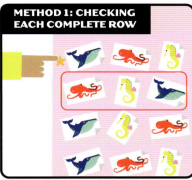

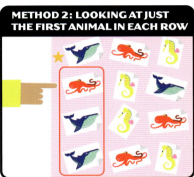

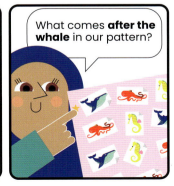

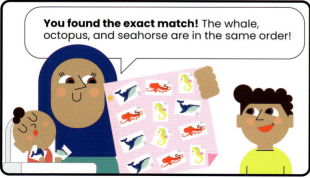

Congratulations!

Celebrate a job well done!

To our Young Pattern Detective: You've done some fantastic work with patterns! Hooray! It's great that you've discovered there's more than one way to solve a pattern puzzle. Whether you checked each row individually or found the matching animal at the start of the row first, you used some important problem-solving skills. You're starting to think like a computer programmer, finding and fixing bugs in code. Keep practising, as these skills will help you solve all kinds of puzzles as you grow.

To the Adult Pattern Detective: There are several key skills your child has practised today, including:
- Pattern recognition and creation
- Decision-making about approach methods
- Problem-solving
- Debugging
- Focus and attention to detail

When finding and then fixing mixed-up patterns, your child is exploring foundational skills that will support future learning in mathematics, coding, and logical thinking, all of which are essential in our fast-paced digital world. The way your child approached the task — whether methodically checking each row or scanning for matching images at the start — shows their natural problem-solving style.

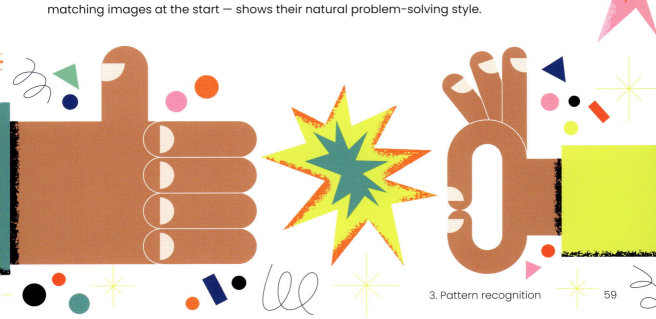

Taking it further

CREATING LONGER PATTERNS

1. Print multiple copies of your chosen images
2. Let the child create their own reference pattern at the top
3. Repeat the pattern in one long line underneath

ORGANISATION METHODS

- Sort the images into separate piles before starting; use the sorted piles to build patterns more efficiently
- Try laying out the first image in each pattern, then the second, then the third
- Experiment with grouping pattern sets into threes
- Let the child discover which organisation method works best

DEBUGGING GAME

4. Start with your reference pattern at the top
5. Create a matching pattern below
6. Have the child close their eyes
7. Move one image out of sequence (start simple)
8. Ask the child to find and fix the mistake
9. Build complexity gradually by moving more images
10. Take turns — let the child create 'bugs' for the adult to find

TEACHING TIPS

- Model positive problem-solving language ("Let's check our pattern.")
- Guide without fixing ("What comes after the whale in our pattern?")
- Let the child choose their organisation strategy
- Break the pattern into groups of three for easier checking
- Celebrate successful debugging
- Make it playful ("Want to trick me with a pattern puzzle?")

Remember: The goal is to build problem-solving skills and confidence in pattern recognition through playful debugging activities.

Activity
Nature walk patterns and debugging

In this activity, we will continue to build on our pattern-creating and debugging skills — what better way to practise pattern debugging than out in the fresh air, using natural objects? This nature walk activity combines collecting natural treasure with learning to spot and fix mistakes in patterns, helping children to develop both critical thinking and navigation abilities.

For younger children, start by creating a simple map with easily identifiable landmarks to follow; the aim is to collect natural items to make patterns with as you go along your route. We will deliberately include some mistakes in our repeating patterns to show children how to approach problem-solving calmly.

Materials and prep

TIME NEEDED

- Set-up: 5 minutes
- Activity: 20–60 minutes, depending on the weather and the child's engagement

REQUIRED

- Suitable seasonal weatherwear
- Paper and pencils/pens for map-making
- Bag for collecting treasure
- Baby wipes and hand sanitiser
- Wrapped sweets for end-of-hunt reward (optional)

PREPARATION

1. Identify local landmarks known to the child
2. Scout the route to ensure that natural items will be available (leaves, twigs, acorns, etc.)
3. Choose an appropriate spot for pattern-making at the end of your treasure hunt
4. Make a copy of the map or take a backup photo

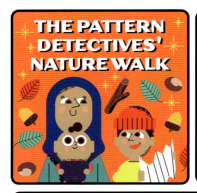

THE PATTERN DETECTIVES' NATURE WALK

Let's go for a walk today and look for some natural treasures to practise our **repeating patterns** with.

OK!

What would you like to find?

Leaves and sticks!

That's awesome. We can try to find acorns and horse chestnuts too. Shall we **make a map** of the park before we go?

YEAH!

Maps, directions, and navigation are explored in more detail in Chapter 7.

Alright, what do we need to make a **map?**

Paper, pen, um...

That's great, well done. What do you know about **landmarks?**

They help us work out where we are.

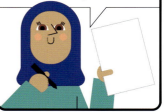

Yes, they do. They also help us work out where we need to go, so we should draw some landmarks to make our map.

Remember, we're looking for natural things today. **Where should we walk first?**

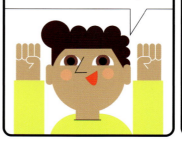

The **bridge!** Then the **bench**, then the **tree**, then the **park!**

Brilliant! You know where you want to go today, don't you!

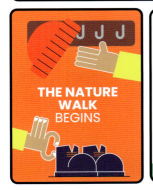

I found some leaves! I found some leaves! They're pretty.

Yes, they're a lovely colour. Well done. Shall we put them in our **treasure bag**?

YES!

Great job, we've reached our **first landmark!** Can you look at the map and tell me what the **next landmark** is, please?

It's the **bench**, come on!

AT THE BENCH...

Look at these, do you know what these are? Can you remember?

No...

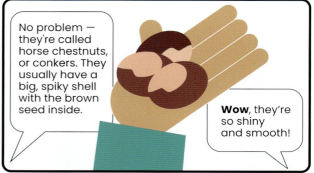

No problem — they're called horse chestnuts, or conkers. They usually have a big, spiky shell with the brown seed inside.

Wow, they're so shiny and smooth!

I know, and sometimes you can get **really big** conkers. Shall we collect some for our **treasure?**

Yes, here you go.

That's a lot of conkers, well done! Where to next, then? Have a look at your **map.**

The tree!

AT THE TREE...

Look at all these sticks! Can we use these as treasure too?

Of course! Let's **collect** some and put them in here.

Yay! I think we need to go to the **park** now.

I think you're right — have a **look at the map to check.** You've collected some awesome treasure already. Well done! When we get to the park, we're going to use our treasure to make **repeating patterns**. Do you want to play on the swings before or after we do our repeating patterns?

After!

PATTERN-MAKING AT THE PARK

AT THE PARK...

So, with all of this treasure here, can you make a **repeating pattern?**

OK. I'm going to do...conker, stick, leaf, conker, stick, leaf, conker, stick...

Great job, well done! What would come after the stick, then?

LEAF!

Yes, well done. Now I'm going to leave your repeating pattern here and **create a different one** using more of our treasure. I want you to close your eyes.

I can't see you!

OK, I'm ready for you to open your eyes now.

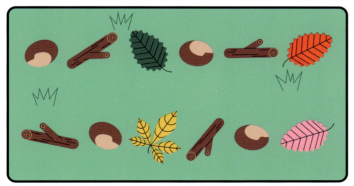

Sometimes we have to do something called **debugging.** You already did some debugging when you remembered to add **home** to our map. Debugging is where we spot something that doesn't look quite right and **fix it.**

Congratulations!

There were a lot of themes for your child to tackle in this activity, so a huge well done to you both for working on these skills.

To our Young Pattern Detective: Wow, fantastic pattern-detecting! You have amazed us grown-ups with your expert map skills, your terrific treasure-hunting skills, and how ace you were at creating, continuing, and debugging repeating patterns. You've learnt some really useful tools that can help you think about how to fix all kinds of things. High five!

To the Adult Pattern Detective: Well done to you and your child for completing this section. You've shown how exploring nature together can lead to exciting discoveries. Using a map to find the way introduces another layer of learning, and this idea can be used in other areas and with other landmarks as well. Looking at patterns, continuing patterns, and debugging patterns will help children tackle all sorts of challenges in the future. Keep exploring and creating patterns in everything you do together. It's lots of fun!

Taking it further

COLLECTION VARIATIONS

- Collect items by colour (green leaves, red leaves, brown nuts, brown sticks)
- Collect items by size or shape (large leaves, skinny twigs, long sticks)
- Collect items by texture (smooth nuts, rough twigs, waxy leaves)
- Create item categories (flat things, thin things, long things, spherical things)
- Look for pairs of matching items

PATTERN CHALLENGES

- Create colour sequences (red leaf, brown stick, orange leaf, red leaf, brown stick, orange leaf)
- Base patterns on size or shape (big leaf, small acorn, big leaf, small acorn)
- Arrange items by texture (rough twigs, waxy leaves, rough twigs, waxy leaves)
- Build shape patterns using natural materials (three sticks to make a triangle, a circle of leaves, repeat)
- Design symmetrical patterns

TEACHING TIPS

- Encourage children to lead the collection process
- Encourage creative categorisation
- Use natural vocabulary (shape, texture, size, etc.)
- Make connections to patterns in nature, using the seasons to your advantage
- Focus on discovery, exploration, and observation
- Keep it playful and fun

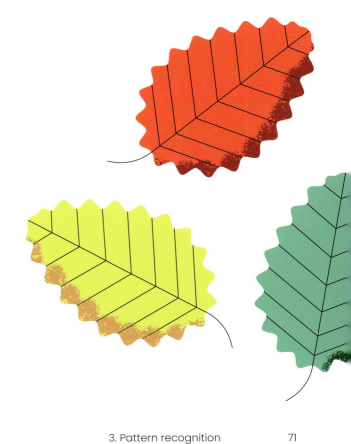

Extension ideas

If your child is enjoying exploring pattern recognition, carry on! Here are some more ideas:

LAUNDRY DAY

- Spot repeating patterns on clothes and other textiles and discuss what comes next in the pattern
- Find a pile of socks and pair them up by matching their patterns
- Hang coloured pegs on clothes in a repeating pattern

HOUSEWORK DAY

- Sort toys into repeating patterns before putting them away: car, dinosaur, unicorn, car, dinosaur, unicorn (this one is perfect for wet-weather play)

Building blocks for coding in Scratch

These pattern recognition activities develop essential pre-coding skills that translate directly into programming in Scratch. When children learn to identify, continue, create, and debug patterns, they're building foundations for:

- **Loop recognition**
  Understanding repeated instructions (like drawing a square using the same code four times)
- **Debugging**
  Using pattern recognition as a more efficient way to spot anomalies in code sequences
- **Logical thinking**
  Planning and predicting outcomes
- **Colour-coding**
  Using visual patterns to organise code blocks

Developing these basic pattern recognition skills facilitates a smoother transition to Scratch programming and helps children progress to other, more complex programming languages as they grow.

4. Algorithms
Following rules and organising instructions

Activities

Essential steps

1. Teach the child to pronounce and understand the word 'algorithm'
2. Show the child how to follow an algorithm
3. Help the child create their own algorithm
4. Have the child demonstrate an algorithm
5. Practice debugging an algorithm together

Success looks like

- Following simple step-by-step instructions
- Using algorithmic language correctly
- Creating basic algorithms for others to follow
- Finding and fixing errors in algorithms

Common challenges

- Too easy → add more steps to the algorithms
- Too hard → use everyday routines as simple algorithms
- Child loses focus → turn algorithms into physical movement games

Introduction

Why algorithms matter

Algorithms are a fundamental part of computational thinking — they help us follow, create, and evolve sets of rules to perform certain actions. While encouraging children to follow rules can be… challenging, it's an essential skill for them to develop! Creating algorithms teaches children to make their instructions as explicit and unambiguous as possible, which takes practice. Through this process, children learn more than just the skills behind working out instructions — they also build vital communication skills. This enables them not only to understand and interpret information given to them but also to articulate their own algorithms to someone or something else, whether that's in their daily activities or, eventually, when computer programming.

Where we see algorithms

Algorithms are everywhere in our daily lives: they can be found in recipes, instruction manuals (LEGO® does this brilliantly), and even mundane tasks like washing dishes or following bedtime routines. These are all examples of tasks with multiple steps that follow specific rules. The key is to notice these natural opportunities to explore algorithms and involve children by casually talking through what you're doing. Whether you're playing board games, following recipes, or completing household tasks, you can introduce algorithmic concepts while doing activities that are already familiar to you and the child. Building on this foundational knowledge helps children understand that algorithms are a normal part of their everyday lives.

How to explain algorithms to children

When talking about algorithms with children, start by introducing this fun mnemonic to help them learn the word itself:

> **Adult:** *"To remember a big word like 'algorithm', we can clap it out. Ready? 'An al-gor-ith-m is a set of rules for us to fol-low.'"*

Once children are comfortable with the word, try these kid-friendly explanations:

> **Adult:** *"Here's a list of instructions — an algorithm is just a list of instructions, a set of rules."*

> **Adult:** *"We have a set of rules here. Do you remember what a set of rules is called? … That's right, an algorithm!"*

Adult: *"To help us make this recipe, we can use this set of instructions here — this algorithm. The algorithm will tell us what to do to make our cake."*

Adult: *"Look at this instruction booklet with all these lovely pictures — these are our rules, our algorithm. If we follow them step by step, we'll have a toy that looks like this at the end! How cool!"*

Activity progress path

Understanding simple sets of instructions is the first step in a child's journey towards developing the ability to follow, create, debug, and share algorithms.

As children progress from observing and following algorithms to creating and debugging their own, they develop critical physical, social, and computational thinking skills.

CORE ACTIVITY: ESTABLISHING AND FOLLOWING A BASIC ALGORITHM

- **Basic**
  Begin with simple moves that can be followed in a set order
- **Intermediate**
  Follow a recipe that ought to produce an expected outcome (fingers crossed!)
- **Advanced**
  Have the child articulate a set of rules for others to follow, encouraging them to debug and refine their instructions

SKILLS DEVELOPMENT

- **Physical**
  Gross motor skills, fine motor skills, spatial awareness
- **Social**
  Collaboration, communication (listening and speaking), sharing
- **Computational**
  Problem decomposition, pattern recognition, logical reasoning, debugging, sequencing

Troubleshooting tips

When introducing children to algorithms, you may face some common challenges. Here's how to handle the situation when your child is:

- **Overwhelmed**
  Start with just two moves for them to copy from you; remove the decision-making at this stage, then try again in a few days, letting them choose their own moves.
- **Frustrated**
  Watch for signs of agitation and share some easier moves to do together. Take breaks if needed.
- **Distracted**
  Remove any discarded toys from view. If necessary, demonstrate how certain toys (like trucks) are less engaging to make moves with than toys with limbs.
- **Losing interest**
  Make it playful — the sillier the moves for the toy, the more fun it is for the child. Don't be afraid to model silly moves yourself (go on, no one's watching!).
- **Showing signs of perfectionism**
  Remind them that we're just having fun with movement algorithms and that it's OK if we mix them up sometimes — we can always try again and keep on learning!

Join **Jack**, **Charlotte**, and **Jordan**
as they turn tasks into
step-by-step adventures!

Activity
Introducing algorithms with dancing toys

Dancing toys are a fun-filled way to teach children about algorithms through movement and play. Using toys with moveable limbs, you'll work together to create, follow, and debug simple dance routines. By creating sequences of dance moves, children learn that algorithms are just step-by-step instructions we can follow.

This activity builds children's listening and speaking skills while introducing them to basic programming concepts. The child will practise following instructions, creating their own sequences, and spotting when moves aren't quite right — all while having fun with their favourite toys!

Materials and prep

TIME NEEDED

- Set-up: 2 minutes
- Activity: 15–45 minutes, depending on the child's engagement

REQUIRED

- Selection of toys with moveable limbs (teddy bears, dolls, action figures)
- Toys without limbs (e.g. trucks and cars) to demonstrate why some toys work better than others (optional)

PREPARATION

1. Clear some floor or table space
2. Select one toy each
3. Review the suggested moves below and choose age-appropriate ones

SUGGESTED MOVES

- Basic:
  - Shake whole toy
  - Nod head
  - Wave arms
  - Jump up and down
- Intermediate:
  - Jump left/right
  - Spin around (360°)
  - Bend forwards/backwards
  - Waggle specific limbs
- Advanced:
  - Stand on head
  - Turn halfway and back (180°)
  - Construct complex limb sequences
  - Combine multiple types of movement

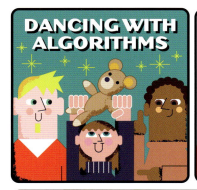

DANCING WITH ALGORITHMS

Let's have fun with your toys and learn about **algorithms**! An algorithm is just a set of steps we follow, like a dance routine.

An al-gor-ith-m is a set of rules for us to fol-low.

CLAP!

Which toy should we use for our dance?

THIS ONE!

Hmm... it'll be tricky without arms and legs!

Maybe we need a different toy?

PETAL!

Perfect! Try copying these dance moves with Petal...

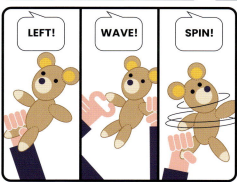

LEFT!

WAVE!

SPIN!

Can I make up the moves?

Of course! That means creating your own algorithm!

Wiggle arm, nod head, spin around!

Was that right? I think we **forgot** something...

No! You missed the head nod!

Good catch! You **debugged our algorithm!**

Learning about algorithms can be as simple as dancing with toys!

Congratulations!

What incredible algorithmic thinking you've shown today! Be sure to celebrate your successes — learning about algorithms is a big achievement.

To our Young Algorithm Innovator: Brilliant work helping your toys learn their dance moves! You've mastered some really important skills today. Not only did you follow algorithms perfectly, but you created your own sequences and even helped spot when moves weren't quite right. That's amazing thinking! You showed that algorithms can be really fun when we use our favourite toys.

To the Adult Algorithm Innovator: Well done for introducing these complex concepts through play! By using familiar toys to teach your child about algorithms, you kept the learning fun and comfortable.

Through this activity, your child has learnt how to:
- Follow algorithms (by understanding someone else's instructions)
- Create algorithms (by making their own sequences)
- Debug algorithms (by spotting and fixing mistakes)

Keep exploring algorithms with your child's toys; try longer sequences and different moves, and have fun making each other giggle when you pretend to forget the next step! Remember, these early foundations in algorithmic thinking help children with everything from maths to basic coding as they grow.

Taking it further

If your child is enjoying this activity, here are some ways to extend
their learning:
- Create longer dance algorithms — add two or three more moves to test the child's memory
- Pair each movement with a unique noise and ask the child to copy them both
- Host a toy disco and have each toy perform their own special algorithm
- Encourage group practice by taking turns being the creator or the follower

DEBUGGING PRACTICE

1. Start with a simple sequence, such as: waggle right arm, nod head, spin around
2. Repeat it with an obvious error: waggle right arm, nod head, spin around, spin around

Remember: By modelling mistakes first, you create a safe space where errors can be seen as learning opportunities. Keep the atmosphere playful and let the child know that it's perfectly fine to try again.

Activity
Biscuit-icing algorithm

Recipes are perfect for teaching children about algorithms — they're simply a series of steps that must be followed in a given order. The task of icing biscuits is particularly good for young children because it's hands-on and visual, and any debugging (fixing of mistakes) always results in something that's still delicious! This activity lets children practise following instructions while also learning that algorithms need to be tested and adjusted.

Materials and prep

TIME NEEDED

- Set-up: 5 minutes
- Activity: 20–45 minutes, depending on the number of biscuits decorated

REQUIRED

- For mixing:
    - Small bowl of icing sugar
    - Small jug of warm water
    - Mixing bowl
    - Tablespoon
    - Teaspoon
    - Paper towels
    - Tablecloth or wipeable surface
- For decorating:
    - Plain biscuits (e.g. digestives or gingerbread men)
    - Sprinkles, chocolate chips, or dried fruit
    - Dessert plate for the finished biscuits
- For learning:
    - Distractor items (socks, pens, toy cars, etc.)

PREPARATION

1. Cover your work surface with the tablecloth
2. Remove unintentional distractions from the workspace
3. Set out the equipment in a logical order
4. Pre-measure three tablespoons of icing sugar into a shallow bowl; keep spare icing sugar nearby (but out of the child's reach)

Note: Measuring the sugar in advance prevents messy sugar clouds from coating everything.

THE ICING ALGORITHM

Do you know how to make **icing for biscuits**? What's the first thing we do?

Um...

We **wash our hands!**

Great job! We also make sure our **surface is clean**. Have you seen us ice anything before?

No, I don't know what you're talking about!

No problem! Icing is that sweet layer we put on cakes, muffins, cookies, or biscuits. It makes them look and taste more interesting.

When it's first made, icing is runny like honey, but then it sets hard. That's how it holds decorations in place.

Like the cakes we have on birthdays?

Exactly!

Let's look at what we need to use to ice our biscuits. We'll **sort** through these things first.

Items we don't want can go on this tray, and then we'll move it to one side. That way, we'll only have what we need.

YAY!

Deconstructing the task helps children to identify what resources they need.

Do you know what **deconstruction** is?

No...

It's when we break a big task into smaller, easier parts.

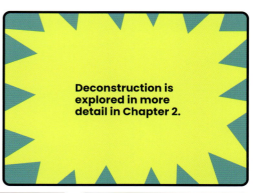

Deconstruction is explored in more detail in Chapter 2.

Would we use a hairbrush to scoop icing sugar?

Yes!

But then we'd get hair in our icing and icing in our hair! What normally helps us scoop things?

A SPOON!

What about this toy car? Is it useful for making icing?

No, we can't eat a toy car!

Right! Might be a bit crunchy!

Continue sorting until only the necessary items remain: bowls, spoons, icing sugar, water, biscuits, and decorations.

Great work! We've **deconstructed** our problem by removing the distractions. Now we can focus on our **algorithm!**

Do you remember what an **algorithm** is? It's just a set of steps we follow, like a recipe.

The icing algorithm:

1. Add two tablespoons of icing sugar to a bowl
2. Add one tablespoon of water
3. Mix together
4. Adjust thickness if needed
5. Spread onto biscuit
6. Add decorations
7. Let icing set
8. Enjoy!

Debugging: when something goes wrong, we fix it.

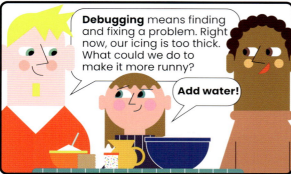

For icing that's too runny, slowly add more icing sugar until it's just right. This teaches important decision-making and problem-solving skills.

Sequencing is explored in more detail in Chapter 5.

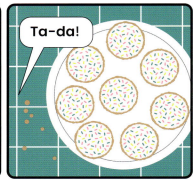

Congratulations!

What amazing progress you've made in algorithmic thinking and problem-solving!

To our Young Algorithm Innovator: Look at those brilliant biscuits you created! You started with plain biscuits and turned them into beautiful treats by following your algorithm step by step. It was fantastic to see how you persevered when things didn't go quite right — that's exactly what computer programmers do! You showed great debugging skills when the icing needed adjusting, and you made lots of lovely patterns with your decorations. Keep practising these skills — they'll help you solve all sorts of challenges as you grow!

To the Adult Algorithm Innovator: This delicious activity demonstrates how a typical baking scenario can be used to explore key computational thinking concepts. Through this hands-on experience, your child has practised:
- Deconstruction (sorting through equipment to find what's needed)
- Algorithmic thinking (following and creating step-by-step instructions)
- Communication (explaining steps clearly to others)
- Debugging (solving problems when the icing wasn't quite right)
- Pattern creation (decorating biscuits in repeating sequences)
- Listening and attention to detail

Though your child thinks they're just having fun baking and decorating (not to mention eating!) biscuits, they're actually building essential foundations for logical thinking and computer programming. These skills will support their future learning when using tools like Scratch. Remember, it's our job to connect the dots between doing fun activities and learning about algorithms, sequencing, and debugging.

Keep exploring these concepts in your everyday activities, and don't forget to enjoy the tasty results of your hard work! The best learning often happens when we're having too much fun to notice we're learning at all.

Taking it further

ORGANISING EQUIPMENT

- Encourage the child to think about what equipment they might use for other activities, like having a bath or making a sandwich
- Experiment with different-sized spoons to help the child develop fine motor skills
- Try different toppings — placing sugar strands individually is good practice when developing a child's fine motor skills; chocolate buttons are a little easier to handle but can (and often will!) melt

THINKING ALGORITHMICALLY

- Let the child take control of the algorithm, using the images as instructions; let them take the lead and instruct you instead
- Ask the child to explain what they did — this bit of memory recall solidifies their learning
- Encourage this type of thinking in other areas

TEACHING TIPS

- Break the whole task down into chunks to make it easier: finding, measuring, making, debugging, decorating, eating
- Model the algorithm from start to finish if you think this will help the child
- Use positive problem-solving language ("Let's see what we did there...")
- Guide without intervention ("What can we do to make our icing runny?")
- Make the icing stiff so that the biscuit snaps during application, then laugh it off — this teaches resilience
- Keep it playful

Activity
Debugging algorithms with cloud dough

Cloud dough is the perfect medium for exploring and debugging algorithms in a hands-on way. Just like following a normal recipe, making cloud dough requires specific steps and often needs adjusting (or *debugging*) to get the right consistency. Together, we'll practise measuring, mixing, and adjusting ingredients to create a dough that can hold its shape.

This activity builds on the child's previous learning while introducing some creative problem-solving opportunities. Though messy, the sensory experience helps make abstract concepts like debugging more concrete and memorable. Through guided discussion and experimentation, children learn that all problems have solutions, and that following steps (or *algorithms*) leads to successful outcomes.

Materials and prep

TIME NEEDED

- Set-up: 5–10 minutes
- Activity: 20–60 minutes, depending on the child's interest

REQUIRED

- For mixing:
  - Cornflour (one cup per person)
  - Hair conditioner (half a cup per person)
  - Large mixing bowls (one per person)
  - Measuring cups
  - Spoons
- For protection:
  - Aprons or old clothes
  - Damp cloth for hands
  - Tablecloth, newspaper, or shower curtain
  - Flat board or plate for rolling
- For decorating:
  - Small buttons and/or beads
  - Twigs and/or fabric scraps
  - Googly eyes

PREPARATION

1. Cover the workspace with your protective layer of choice
2. Set out individual mixing bowls
3. Pre-measure four cups of cornflour into a large bowl
4. Prepare the decorative materials and keep them nearby (but out of the way for now)
5. Have extra cornflour and conditioner ready for debugging

THE CLOUD DOUGH ALGORITHM

Let's make **cloud dough!** First, I'll read through our algorithm — that's just like a recipe or a set of steps for us to follow. Ready?

Ready!

Cloud dough recipe

1. Add half a cup of hair conditioner to a bowl
2. Gently mix in one cup of cornflour (careful — it can puff!)
3. Mix until a dough forms
4. Adjust consistency if needed:
   • Too dry ➤ add more conditioner
   • Too wet ➤ add more cornflour
5. Knead until smooth

Let's add the conditioner first.

Is this enough?

Perfect!

Now for the tricky part... we need to add the cornflour **very** gently.

See how it makes a little cloud? That's why we **do it slowly.**

Like this?

Perfect! Nice and gentle.

Now we **mix** until it looks like dough.

It's really hard!

Let's check our **instructions.**

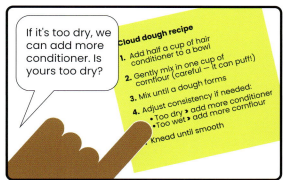

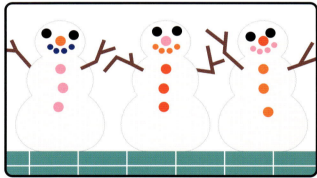

Congratulations!

What fantastic algorithmic thinking and problem-solving you've done today!

To our Young Problem Detector: Brilliant work following the algorithm and making sure each step was in the correct sequence! You showed amazing debugging skills when things didn't go quite right. When your snowman toppled over, you didn't give up — you tried again and worked out that the biggest ball needs to go at the bottom. That's called perseverance, and it's a super important skill to have when solving all kinds of problems. Well done for keeping going even when things got tricky!

To the Adult Problem Detector: Well done for embracing the messy fun that is cloud dough! Through this playful activity, your child has learnt how to:

- Follow algorithms
- Debug algorithms
- Sequence tasks
- Persevere

Although this activity involved complex concepts, exploring them through hands-on play helped make them more accessible and memorable. By encouraging creative freedom, you introduced opportunities for communication and collaboration. These early experiences with algorithms, sequencing, and debugging will help your child develop critical thinking skills that they'll continue to use throughout their lives.

Keep exploring these concepts through everyday activities, and remember to celebrate those debugging successes!

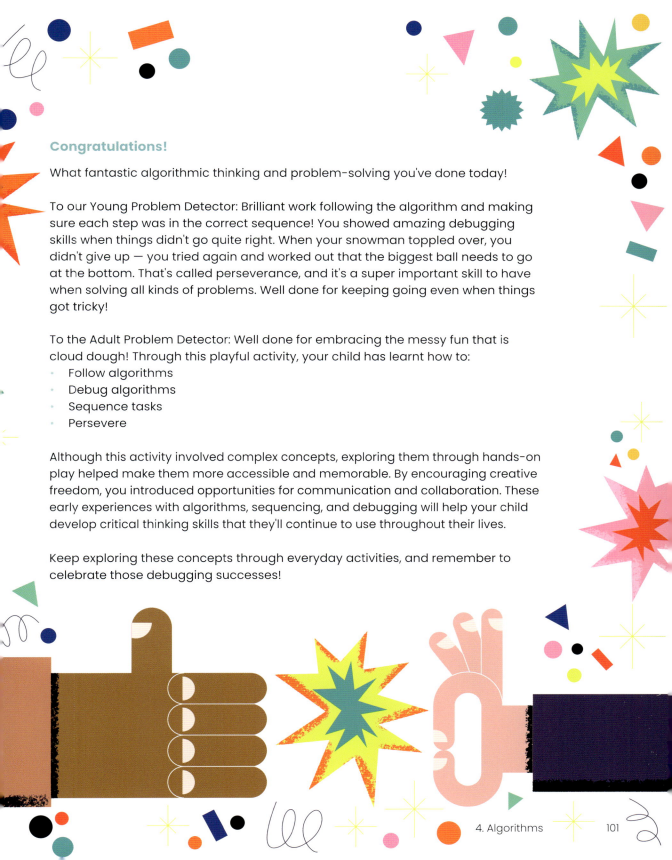

Taking it further

ALGORITHM VARIATIONS

- Draw pictures to tick off as you complete each step
- Let the child lead the process, using the pictures as instructions
- Discuss how you'd explain these steps to a robot or an alien
- Adjust the amounts to make larger quantities
- Add food colouring for more creative play (mix with conditioner first)

SEQUENCING CHALLENGES

- Practise the proper order when adding ingredients
- Discuss the order when decorating cloud dough models
- Talk about why each sequence matters (like adding food colouring early to avoid stained hands)

CLOUD DOUGH EXPLORATION

- Try different conditioner scents for sensory play
- Challenge the child to make small and large creations
- Make imprints with toys and natural objects
- Create recognisable items for others to guess
- Create shapes and repeating patterns (using cutters to make them consistent)

TEACHING TIPS

- Encourage self-direction with the algorithm
- Only intervene when necessary
- Use computational vocabulary (algorithm, sequencing, debugging)
- Make connections to everyday objects
- Focus on creativity and experimentation
- Keep things fun while still prioritising algorithmic thinking

Note: Cloud dough can be stored in a plastic box for several weeks. Dispose of it in your general waste bin when finished.

Extension ideas

If your child is enjoying learning about algorithms, here are some other, more skill-oriented ideas:

- **Maths**
  Make shapes with the cloud dough and arrange them in size order
- **Science**
  Create a basic 2D model of the human body and identify different body parts
- **Sensory**
  Mould the dough into shapes that match the conditioner's scent (e.g. apples)

Building blocks for coding in Scratch

These activities teach children about algorithms by applying rules and processes to familiar tasks. When children learn to follow, create, articulate (verbally or through drawings), and debug rules, they're also building foundations for:

- **Algorithmic thinking**
  Understanding and applying programming logic and language
- **Debugging**
  Using steps to identify where problems occurred and how to fix them
- **Sequencing**
  Using order to establish the best way to achieve the desired outcome

Learning these computational thinking skills early makes for an easier transition to Scratch programming.

5. Sequencing
Understanding order

Activities

Essential steps

1. Select a multi-step activity
2. Show the child the steps involved
3. Guide the child to complete each step in the sequence
4. Mix up the sequence and ask the child to rearrange it in proper order

Success looks like

- Completing the steps in a sequence
- Creating a sequence
- Debugging a sequence

Common challenges

- Too easy → introduce a more complex sequence
- Too hard → create a sequence with just two or three steps
- Child loses focus → incorporate toys, singing, or dancing

Introduction

Why sequencing matters

We naturally follow all kinds of sequences as we go about our day. While adults manage these sequences automatically, children are still discovering how tasks fit together in the right order. This understanding becomes especially important when working with computers, where instructions must be given in exactly the right sequence to achieve the desired result. Teaching children to spot and follow sequences equips them with the computational thinking skills to effectively tackle their tasks, whether they're following stories, creating music, solving mathematical problems, or programming computers.

Where we see sequencing

Sequences are everywhere in our daily lives. We can use familiar activities to teach children about sequences in a low-stakes way, like when we're following recipes (first mix, then bake), getting dressed (socks before shoes!), or playing our favourite games. This helps them understand that sometimes things need to happen in a specific order to work properly — even the fun stuff! The more we draw attention to sequencing in our daily activities, the more natural it becomes for children to break down tasks into logically ordered steps.

How to explain sequencing to children

When talking about sequencing with children, try these kid-friendly explanations:

> **Adult:** *"A sequence is about following steps in order, just like when we're getting ready for bed. First we put on pyjamas, then we brush our teeth, then we read a story."*

> **Adult:** *"While an algorithm is a set of rules that tells us what to do, a sequence tells us the order we need to do those things in."*

Applying the concept to familiar scenarios encourages children to interact with the idea:

> **Adult:** *"Sometimes the order we do things in really matters. What would happen if you didn't follow the sequence for bathtime and only took your clothes off after you got in the bath?"*

> **Child:** *"My clothes would get wet!"*

> **Adult:** *"That's right! When we follow a sequence, each step leads us on to the next one! Sometimes we might get the steps mixed up, but that's OK — we can fix it and try again."*

Continue to use everyday activities to demonstrate sequences. Point out words like 'first', 'next', 'then', and 'after' to help children understand order. If something goes wrong, treat it as a fun opportunity to problem-solve together.

Activity progress path

Understanding simple sequences is the first step in a child's journey towards developing the ability to follow, create, share, and debug sequences of all complexities. These skills are essential to their daily life experiences as well as any future computer programming endeavours.

When children observe adults performing sequences, they learn critical skills that enable them to create and perform their own. Working together, adults and children can communicate and collaborate to establish the best sequence for any given situation. While debugging sequences, children apply both social and computational thinking skills to real-life experiences, developing the problem-solving abilities they will come to rely on in their personal lives and careers.

CORE ACTIVITY: ESTABLISHING AND FOLLOWING SEQUENCES

- **Basic**
  Begin with simple sequences, like watching a grown-up unlock and open the front door
- **Intermediate**
  Follow multi-step sequences, such as rainbow colours and pedestrian crossing rules
- **Advanced**
  Debug incorrect sequences when adults perform them wrong, explaining what needs fixing

SKILLS DEVELOPMENT

- **Physical**
  Gross motor skills, fine motor skills, observation
- **Social**
  Collaboration, communication (listening and speaking)
- **Computational**
  Algorithms, logical reasoning, debugging

Troubleshooting tips

When helping children learn about sequences, you may face some common challenges. Here's how to handle the situation when your child is:

- **Overwhelmed**
  Break the sequence into smaller parts; start with just two or three steps for more familiar activities, like putting on shoes or brushing teeth. Build up to longer sequences gradually.

- **Frustrated**
  Watch for early signs of stress and suggest a movement break. Acting out the sequence with whole-body movements can help release tension and reinforce their learning.

- **Distracted**
  Keep the workspace clear and tidy — have only the materials needed for your current sequence visible. Store other items out of sight.

- **Rushing**
  Stay calm and turn mistakes into debugging opportunities: "Let's check if our sequence works... Oops, we missed a step! Shall we debug it together, like computer programmers do?"

- **Losing interest**
  Make it playful — turn sequences into silly games, like "What happens if we brush our teeth before putting toothpaste on the brush?"

- **Showing signs of perfectionism**
  Remind them that debugging is an important part of both learning and computing — even professional programmers need to fix their sequences sometimes!

Learn how to put things
in the right order with
Katie and **Aisha**!

Activity
Rainbow sequence

Learning about rainbows is the perfect introduction to sequencing. Just as computers follow sequences of instructions, rainbows always display their colours in the same order. By spotting and fixing incorrect rainbow sequences, children learn to problem-solve as they would when debugging computer code.

Through hands-on activities like sorting coloured pom-poms with tweezers or finding rainbow-coloured objects around the house, children develop both sequencing skills and fine motor control. For younger children, this activity also builds core skills in colour recognition and counting.

Materials and prep

TIME NEEDED

- Set-up: 5 minutes
- Activity: Approx. 15 minutes, depending on the child's engagement

REQUIRED

- Plain paper or card
- Rainbow-coloured drawing implements (crayons, chalks, pens, or pencils)
- Alternative rainbow-coloured materials for extension activities (e.g. foam shapes, LEGO/DUPLO bricks, mini pom-poms, or pegs)
- Clear, flat surface to work on

PREPARATION

1. Clear a dedicated workspace
2. Remove any distractions
3. Gather enough items to create a complete rainbow sequence
4. Have alternative materials ready (but keep them out of sight)
5. Warm up those singing voices for the rainbow song!

RAINBOW PATTERN QUEST

Can you see that amazing **rainbow** over there?

Yes! It's so pretty!

Begin with real-world observation and questioning.

Do you know how rainbows are made?

With water and sunshine?

That's right! When it's showery and sunny, the sun shines through tiny water drops in the air.

Simplify and introduce complex concepts.

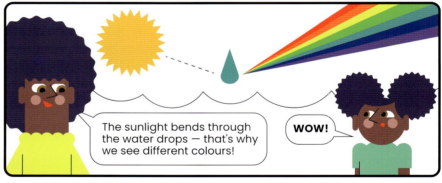

The sunlight bends through the water drops — that's why we see different colours!

WOW!

Do you remember all the **rainbow colours?**

Red... and **yellow**... but I forget the others.

Let's use our special saying then: **Really Old Yoghurt Goes Bad In Vans!**

That's funny! What does it mean?

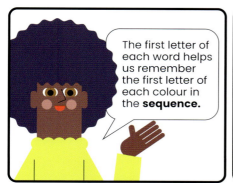

The first letter of each word helps us remember the first letter of each colour in the **sequence.**

Really...

Really for **red!** Like a fire engine!

Old...

Old for **orange!** Like an orange!

Yoghurt...

Yellow! Like the sun!

Goes...

Goes means **green!** Like grass!

Bad...

Bad is **blue!** Like the sky!

In...

In for **indigo!** That's dark blue!

Vans!

Violet! Like the flower

Use multiple learning approaches.

Let's check our work against this picture of a real rainbow. Can you point to each colour?

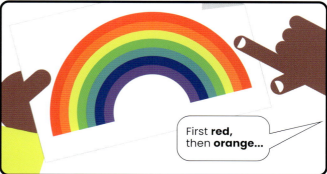

First **red,** then **orange...**

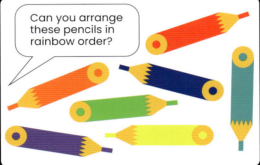

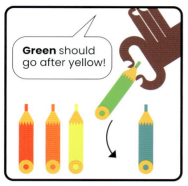

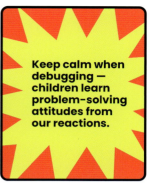

Congratulations!

What brilliant sequence spotting you did whilst learning about rainbows.

To our Young Rainbow Creator: Brilliant work with those rainbow colours! You mastered the sequence and learnt how to spot when things weren't quite right. Just like a computer programmer, you can now follow steps in order and fix mistakes when they happen. Keep watching for rainbows when it's sunny and rainy — you're becoming an expert rainbow detective!

To the Adult Rainbow Creator: Through playful rainbow exploration, your child has learnt about some important computing concepts, including:
- Algorithms (understanding rainbow conditions)
- Sequencing (mastering ROYGBIV order)
- Debugging (fixing incorrect sequences)

These foundational skills will support them in their future coding activities, especially when they start to explore programs like Scratch. Whether they're creating sequences or fixing mixed-up ones, your child is building essential problem-solving skills that can eventually be developed into real computing abilities.

Keep on exploring rainbows together, and watch out for those special double rainbows that appear when conditions are perfect!

Taking it further

RAINBOW VARIATIONS

- Draw rainbows using different line styles (wavy, zigzag, straight)
- Create rainbow collages from magazine pictures
- Make rainbow greeting cards for loved ones
- Make rainbow sequences with different household objects

MOVEMENT AND MUSIC

- Perform the rainbow song with a sequence of movements
- Present rainbow sequences to a soft toy audience; let favourite toys watch rainbow demonstrations
- Keep the learning playful and fun

DEBUGGING GAME

1. Create a reference rainbow sequence at the top
2. Make a matching sequence below
3. Have the child close their eyes while you rearrange the matching sequence
4. Ask the child to identify and fix the incorrect sequence; use humour when discussing the wrong colours
5. Switch roles — let the child create sequences for you to debug

ORGANISATION ACTIVITY

1. Gather all the colouring pencils at your disposal
2. Find and select just the colours included in the rainbow
3. Use the sorted colours to build sequences

POM-POM ACTIVITY

Materials needed:
- Rainbow-coloured pom-poms
- Shallow containers or trays
- Plastic tweezers (optional)

Steps:
1. Sort pom-poms by colour in the first container
2. Using tweezers (or fingers to practise pincer grip), transfer the pom-poms into another container one by one to create a rainbow sequence
3. Check the sequence against the ROYGBIV pattern
4. Mix the pom-poms up and repeat

Activity
Pedestrian crossing light sequence

Turn a simple walk into an engaging lesson about sequences and safety. This activity helps children understand how traffic signals work through hands-on practice at home, followed by real-world application. By breaking down the crossing sequence into clear and concise steps, children can learn about essential computing concepts while developing road safety awareness.

Materials and prep

TIME NEEDED

- Set-up: 10 minutes
- Activity: 10–45 minutes, depending on the child's interest

REQUIRED

- 9 lolly/ice pop sticks (or paper strips, 2 cm × 10 cm in size)
- Felt-tip pens (black, red, green, orange)
- Plain A4 (or letter) paper

PREPARATION

Note: The following setup is for pedestrian crossings in the UK. If you live in a different country, you will likely need a different set of coloured sticks.

1. Create the pedestrian signals:
   a. 2 sticks with a red standing figure
   b. 1 stick with a green walking figure
   c. 1 stick with 'beep, beep, beep' text
2. Create the traffic signals:
   a. 1 stick with red and orange circles
   b. 1 stick with an orange circle
   c. 1 stick with a red circle
   d. 1 stick with a green circle

You will also need a stick with a black button or circle to use as your traffic light button.

3. Clear the workspace of distractions
4. Position the materials within easy reach

These simple props help children understand how computers use sequences to control traffic systems, making learning both fun and interactive.

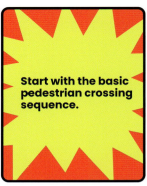

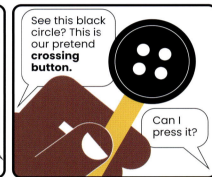

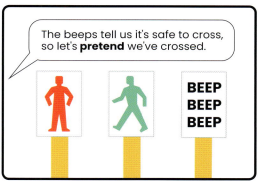

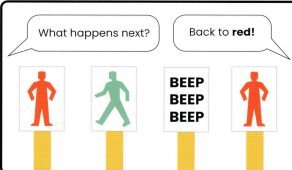

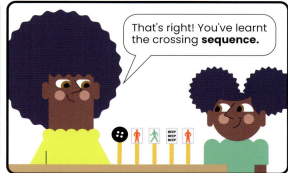

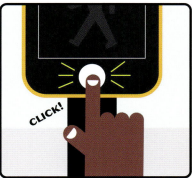

What's happening now?

The green person and the beeping are telling us to go!

Even with the green person and beeping, we always **look both ways**. Why?

To make sure the cars have **stopped!**

That's right — our eyes and ears keep us safe!

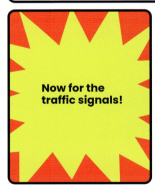

Now for the traffic signals!

BACK AT HOME

Ready to learn something new? These sticks show us what the cars see!

More colours!

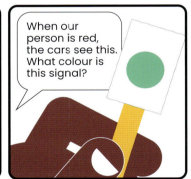

When our person is red, the cars see this. What colour is this signal?

Green! Green means **go!**

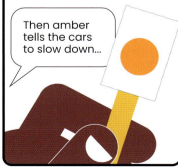

Then amber tells the cars to slow down...

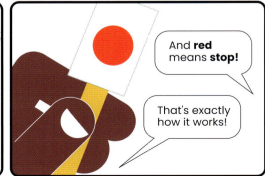

And **red** means **stop!**

That's exactly how it works!

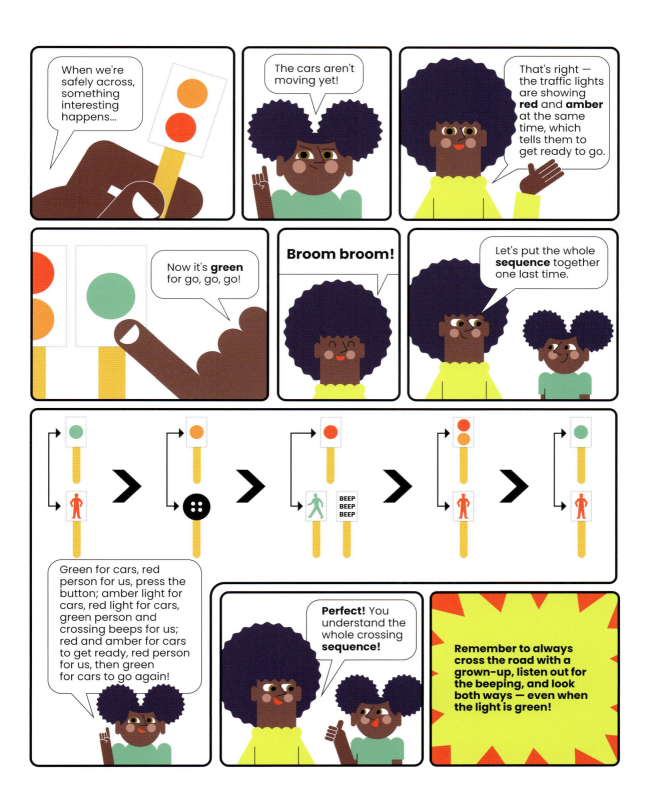

Congratulations!

What a brilliant achievement in learning about sequencing and road safety!

To our Young Road Safety Expert: Fantastic work with the crossing sequence! You're thinking like a computer programmer already — following steps carefully and checking for mistakes. Everything you've learnt about traffic lights and crossing signals will help you understand lots of other sequences as you grow.

Remember: Always cross at proper crossings and hold an adult's hand.

To the Adult Road Safety Expert: Your child has practised several key skills in this activity, including:

- Sequencing (creating and following ordered steps)
- Debugging (finding solutions when sequences don't work)
- Algorithmic thinking (understanding road rules and signals)
- Pattern recognition (noticing repeating signal patterns)

When working through the crossing sequence, your child also learnt about cause and effect (pressing the button makes the lights change) and how to follow precise steps. While crossing may seem routine to adults, to children it's a chance to discover how the world works.

Well done to you both!

Taking it further

SEQUENCE MASTERY

- Create a reference crossing sequence on some paper
- Take turns practising the sequence — adult guides child, then child guides adult
- Practise reciting the sequence with eyes closed — one person directs while the other follows with lolly sticks
- Move the lolly sticks across the workspace to show progression through the steps
- Once well-practised, try reciting the sequence from memory

GETTING ORGANISED

- Sort the equipment into clear groups before starting
- Give children special roles like 'button presser' or 'crossing announcer'
- Use directional language when spotting crossings during outings (this will help with the activities in Chapter 7: Maps, Directions, and Navigation)

DEBUGGING GAME

1. Display the crossing sequence for reference
2. Set up a matching sequence with the lolly sticks
3. Have the child close their eyes while you move or remove one stick; start simple, then try more complex changes
4. Ask the child to identify the missing or moved step
5. Take turns creating and solving sequence puzzles
6. Always review the correct sequence after debugging

TEACHING TIPS

- Use encouraging problem-solving language
- Guide with questions rather than corrections
- Let children develop their own organisation methods
- Break the sequences into smaller chunks if needed
- Celebrate successful debugging
- Keep the activities playful and fun
- Focus on building confidence through play, and patience at real crossings

Remember: The goal is to help children develop sequencing skills and road safety awareness through enjoyable debugging activities that mirror how computers follow and check instructions.

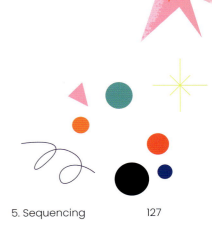

Activity
Debugging a getting-dressed sequence

Getting dressed independently is an important skill for children to develop. This activity adds a fun computational thinking twist, helping children to practise communication, sequencing, and problem-solving too. By discussing and working out the order in which we typically put on clothes, children learn to apply logical reasoning to their everyday tasks.

Remember to keep things playful and to be a bit silly — it makes learning more fun! This activity can easily be adapted to suit different seasons or occasions (like nursery, walks, or swimming), creating natural opportunities for new discussions about sequencing and appropriate clothing choices.

Materials and prep

TIME NEEDED

- Set-up: 5 minutes
- Activity: 15–45 minutes, depending on the child's engagement

REQUIRED

- Basic clothing:
  - Underwear and vest
  - Socks
  - Leggings or trousers
  - T-shirt or top
  - Jumper (sweater)
  - Footwear
  - Accessories (optional)
- Seasonal and outdoor items:
  - Summer gear (sun hat, sunglasses, sandals)
  - Winter gear (coat, boots, gloves, hat, scarf)
  - Wet-weather gear (waterproof jacket, umbrella)

PREPARATION

1. Clear a space near the child's clothes storage
2. Remove distractions from the area
3. Choose weather-appropriate clothing items
4. Lay out the items where the child can easily see them
5. Ensure the items are within the child's reach

DEBUG THE DRESS-UP

It's time to get dressed! Let's find your **clothes.**

Sure!

Can I wear my purple jumper?

Here's a **vest**, a top, your purple jumper, your underwear, a **vest**, your socks, and some trousers.

You picked two **vests!**

You just **debugged** our first problem! We would have been very confused.

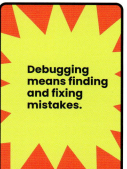

Debugging means finding and fixing mistakes.

Let's arrange everything and plan out our **sequence.**

I want to put my **jumper** on first — I'm cold!

What always goes under a **jumper?**

T-shirt!

And under that?

A **vest!** Remember the two vests?

Learning to get dressed encourages independence; laughing together makes it fun and memorable!

Congratulations!

Excellent exploring the sequence of getting dressed and how we can debug our sequence if we need to/when things go awry!

To our Young Getting-Ready Champion: Fantastic work with your clothing sequences! You've mastered placing clothes in order, thinking about what goes on when, and solving tricky dressing puzzles. You've learnt some wonderful skills that will help you fix all sorts of problems — and you had fun doing it! Your brain has worked hard today learning about sequences, and you should feel very proud.

To the Adult Getting-Ready Guide: Well done for turning the everyday task of getting dressed into an exciting learning adventure. You've shown how daily activities can teach us important skills while still allowing us to have fun together. Through play, your child has explored:
- Sequencing (creating and following dressing orders)
- Debugging (finding solutions when clothes are mixed up)
- Algorithms (understanding clothing layer rules)
- Patterns (recognising daily dressing routines)

When working out dressing sequences and fixing mixed-up clothes, your child is developing essential computational thinking skills that will support their learning in mathematics, coding, and logical thinking. Whether they carefully lay out their clothes first or jump straight into solving problems, your child is already beginning to demonstrate their natural problem-solving style.

Remember to encourage the funny moments — like discovering why T-shirts go under jumpers, not over them! These playful discoveries make the learning stick and show our children why sequences matter. Keep exploring, keep debugging, and keep celebrating each success together.

Taking it further

BUILDING INDEPENDENCE

- Draw the clothing items in sequence and tick them off as the child dresses themselves
- Create visual sequence charts for their wardrobe
- Practise daily before big changes, like starting school
- Adjust the amount of adult help gradually as the child's confidence grows

ORGANISATION SKILLS

- Sort through the clothes to practise categorisation
- Use positional language ('in the bottom drawer', 'on the hook by the door')
- Count the items while getting dressed

WEATHER-WISE DRESSING

- Check the weather before choosing clothes: think about keeping warm, cool, or dry
- Sort clothes by seasons
- Play around with silly choices ("It's snowing today! Should we wear our swimming costumes or our winter coats?")

DEBUGGING PRACTICE

- Fix backwards clothes by starting again; let the child figure out that they can turn a T-shirt around without taking it off
- Sort clothes so they're the right way round before starting
- Test different dressing sequences

TEACHING TIPS

- Guide without fixing ("What comes next?")
- Keep it playful ("Oh no, my hat's covering my eyes!")
- Practise tricky skills separately
- Stay patient during debugging moments

Extension ideas

If your child is enjoying these activities, here are some more ways to explore sequencing together:

SPECIAL OCCASIONS

- Pack a swimming bag in sequence
- Plan clothes for a park adventure
- Sort beach-day items in order
- Arrange party clothes

EVERYDAY SEQUENCES

- Pack a school bag in sequence
- Plan morning activities
- Follow a bedtime routine
- Follow recipe steps in order

NATURAL WORLD SEQUENCES

- Talk about the sequence of day and night
- Talk about the changing seasons
- Observe weather patterns
- Plant seeds and watch them grow
- Learn about butterfly life cycles

Building blocks for coding in Scratch

These sequencing activities develop essential pre-coding skills that lend themselves directly to learning how to program. When children practise planning, creating, and debugging sequences, they're also laying the foundations for:

- **Logical thinking**
  Planning steps and predicting outcomes
- **Critical thinking**
  Improving processes through testing
- **Algorithmic thinking**
  Creating clear, ordered instructions
- **Debugging**
  Finding and fixing problems

Developing these early sequencing skills makes the transition to Scratch programming more natural and fun. When children understand how everyday sequences work, they're better prepared for any coding adventures ahead.

6. Logic
Thinking through problems and making reasoned decisions

Activities

Essential steps

1. Choose a logical thinking challenge (e.g. stacking, sorting, planning)
2. Demonstrate how to think through the problem
3. Guide the child to test their solution
4. Encourage trying different approaches when the first attempt doesn't work

Success looks like

- Making reasoned choices
- Testing and evaluating solutions
- Learning from unsuccessful attempts
- Explaining their thinking process

Common challenges

- Too easy → add more variables or complexity to the problem
- Too hard → break the challenge into simpler parts
- Child loses focus → transform the challenge into a game or story

Introduction

Why logic matters

Logical thinking is a fundamental skill that not only helps us make sense of the world but also to make better decisions. It's the ability to analyse situations, weigh up options, and think through consequences before taking action. When children develop their logical reasoning, they gain confidence in solving problems and communicating their ideas clearly; these skills are essential in everything they do, from daily routines and schoolwork to other, more complex challenges. Just as computers use logic to process information and make decisions, children who understand how to think logically are better prepared for the future — whether they're planning a project, solving a maths problem, or learning how to code.

Where we see logic

Logic is woven throughout our daily lives, and we can help children discover its power through simple questions about everyday decisions. Just as computers use 'if-then' statements to make choices, we naturally use logic when deciding how to answer questions like "Is it bright enough for sunglasses?" or "Do we need an umbrella?"

Children develop logical thinking by observing how we break down problems and make decisions. Whether they're planning a shopping list, choosing appropriate clothes for the day's weather, or sorting their toys, these simple activities help build the same logical reasoning skills that computers use to process information. Making these connections explicit helps children understand how logic works in both digital and real-world problem-solving scenarios.

How to explain logic to children

When talking to children about logic, try these kid-friendly explanations:

> **Adult:** "Before we start painting our butterfly, what should we do first? Choose our colours, fold the paper, or draw the outline? Let's think about what makes the most sense."

> **Adult:** "We need milk, bread, and cereal. Which should we put in our basket first? Remember, milk is heavy — would it make sense to carry it around the whole shop?"

> **Adult:** "Look at your puddle suit and these different pairs of shoes. Which pair would work best for splashing in puddles? Why?"

Adult: *"Oops, we've lost our shopping list! Let's think about this step by step. What did we have for breakfast this morning? That might help us remember what we need."*

Activity progress path

Understanding how to apply logic to everyday activities is an important step in a child's journey towards developing sophisticated problem-solving skills. By encouraging children to think through situations rather than giving them immediate answers, we can help them strengthen their reasoning abilities.

As children progress from following adult-guided reasoning to independently solving problems and debugging challenges, they develop essential physical, social, and computational thinking skills that naturally facilitate future coding experiences.

CORE ACTIVITY: THINKING LOGICALLY AND DEBUGGING PROBLEMS

- **Basic**
  Review and assess situations, using trial and error to work out solutions (like building stable towers or choosing appropriate clothing)
- **Intermediate**
  Make independent logical decisions, such as planning painting steps or choosing the order of shopping items
- **Advanced**
  Debug unexpected problems, like lost shopping lists or paint transfer issues, and articulate the reasoning clearly

SKILLS DEVELOPMENT

- **Physical**
  Fine motor skills, spatial awareness, organisation
- **Social**
  Collaboration, communication, patience, emotional regulation
- **Computational**
  Logical reasoning, debugging, sequencing, problem decomposition

Troubleshooting tips

When introducing children to logical thinking, you may face some common challenges. Here's how to handle the situation when your child is:

- **Overwhelmed**
  Start with simple either/or choices: "Should we put the big box or the small box at the bottom?" Break down decisions into clear options before moving to more complex reasoning.
- **Frustrated**
  Watch for signs of agitation when solving problems; take a quick break and return with a simpler challenge that builds confidence.
- **Distracted**
  Keep the workspace clear and focused on the current activity. With shopping activities, create shorter lists and shop at quieter times.
- **Rushing**
  Channel their enthusiasm into practising step-by-step thinking: "Let's pause and think about what might happen next." Model careful consideration of choices.
- **Losing interest**
  Make logical thinking playful: turn choices into games, create silly decision-making scenarios, or add movement to thinking tasks.
- **Showing signs of perfectionism**
  Emphasise that trying different solutions helps us learn. Share examples of when you had to think through multiple options to solve a problem.

Think through problems and
make smart choices with
Alan, **Ben**, and **Sarah**!

Activity
Tumbling towers

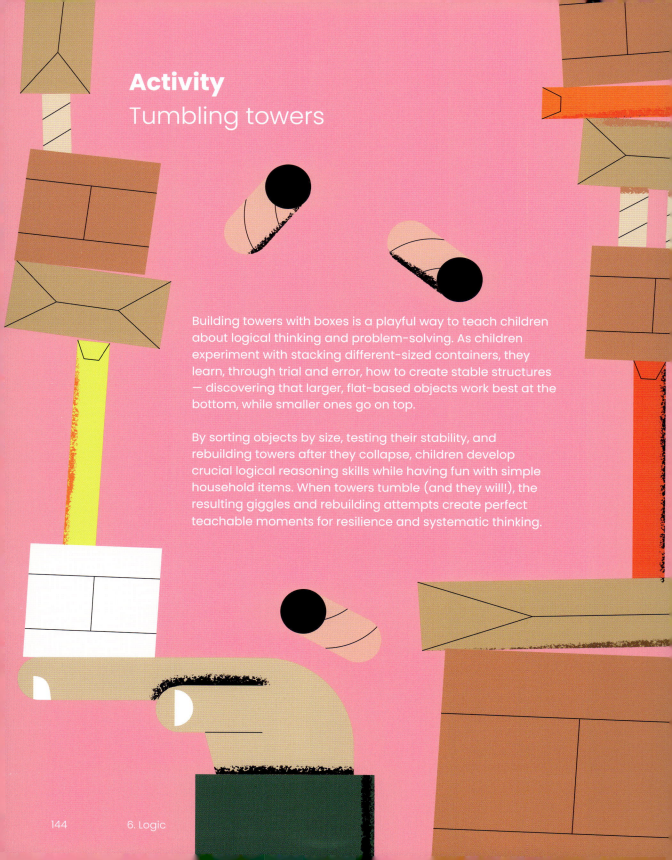

Building towers with boxes is a playful way to teach children about logical thinking and problem-solving. As children experiment with stacking different-sized containers, they learn, through trial and error, how to create stable structures — discovering that larger, flat-based objects work best at the bottom, while smaller ones go on top.

By sorting objects by size, testing their stability, and rebuilding towers after they collapse, children develop crucial logical reasoning skills while having fun with simple household items. When towers tumble (and they will!), the resulting giggles and rebuilding attempts create perfect teachable moments for resilience and systematic thinking.

Materials and prep

TIME NEEDED

- Set-up: 5 minutes
- Activity: 15–45 minutes, depending on the child's engagement

REQUIRED

- Selection of cardboard boxes (delivery boxes, cereal boxes, tissue boxes, etc.)
- Toilet roll tubes
- Different types of containers (plastic cups, bowls)
- Paper and pencils for planning (optional)
- Clear floor space for building

PREPARATION

1. Save various boxes ahead of time
2. Clear some dedicated floor space
3. Remove nearby distractions
4. Consider size order of boxes before starting
5. Start with just three items before adding more

Top tips: Begin with three stable boxes to build the child's confidence, then gradually introduce more challenging shapes. The floor works better than a table for this activity.

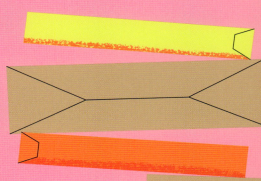

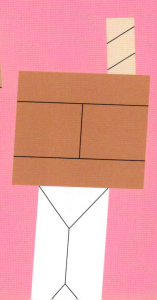

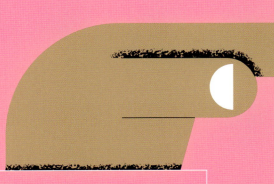

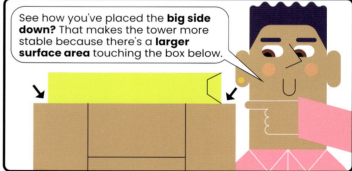

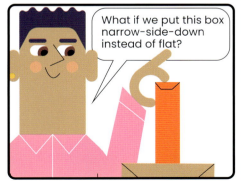

Congratulations!

What an amazing journey you've shared, building towers and solving problems together!

To our Young Tower Builder: Brilliant work becoming an expert builder! You've shown great skill in choosing the right boxes, creating stable structures, and solving problems when the towers toppled. You've learnt that sometimes the best way to build a tall tower is to think carefully about each piece before placing it. Keep using these skills whenever you tackle a tricky task — remember how you made towers stronger by putting bigger boxes at the bottom!

To the Adult Tower Builder: Great job helping your child discover some valuable engineering and problem-solving skills through play. This tower-building adventure has taught them about:
- Logical reasoning (choosing the right boxes for stability)
- Sequencing (ordering boxes by size and structure)
- Algorithms (following steps to build successful towers)
- Collaboration (working together to solve problems)

Keep reinforcing these thinking skills in your everyday activities — whether you're stacking blocks, organising toys, or tackling new construction challenges. Remember, every time you help your child think through a building problem, you're developing their confidence in logical thinking. These skills will help them approach future challenges with strategy and creativity!

Taking it further

BUILDING VARIATIONS

- Test different cardboard thicknesses
- Stack non-flat objects (round containers, irregular shapes)
- Create patterns by colour or size
- Add toys as decorative toppers
- Practise careful placement to develop fine motor skills

DEBUGGING EXTENSIONS

- Document successful and unsuccessful towers through drawings
- Compare stable and unstable structures
- Explain building strategies to an audience of soft toys
- Make intentional mistakes to spark discussion
- Model positive problem-solving language

SEQUENTIAL THINKING

- Order the boxes by size before building
- Count the boxes in the successful towers
- Create repeating patterns
- Turn building into an instructional game

TEACHING OPPORTUNITIES

- Let the child select and sort materials
- Encourage a broad size vocabulary ('largest', 'smaller', 'smallest')
- Make connections to real-world structures
- Focus on discovery through trial and error

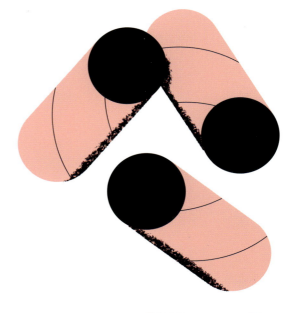

Activity
Symmetrical butterfly paintings

Create beautiful symmetrical butterflies and explore cause and effect using paint and paper folding. This creative activity introduces children to logical thinking as they experiment with colour placement and paint quantities. While children have complete creative freedom with the colours, they learn that they must follow a systematic approach to achieve symmetry. This helps teach them that even artistic results often come from careful planning.

Materials and prep

TIME NEEDED

- Set-up: 5 minutes
- Activity: 15–45 minutes, depending on the child's engagement

REQUIRED

- White A4 (or letter) paper
- Washable paint
- Paintbrushes and palette (a clean cereal box works well)
- Cup of water for rinsing the brushes
- Protective covering for the work surface (newspaper or tablecloth)
- Aprons or old clothes
- Scissors and pencils
- Cleaning supplies (wipes, damp cloth)

OPTIONAL

- A4 card
- Glue

PREPARATION

1. Clear the area of any items you don't want painted
2. Cover the work surface with your protective covering
3. Put on protective clothing
4. Gather cleaning supplies
5. Check paint pots open easily
6. Set out small amounts of paint
7. Create an example butterfly (optional)

BASIC STEPS

1. Fold the paper in half
2. Paint half a butterfly on one side
3. Press the paper halves together
4. Reveal your symmetrical butterfly
5. Debug (if needed) by adding more paint

THE SYMMETRICAL BUTTERFLY

Today we're making butterflies, but not just any butterflies — **symmetrical** ones!

What's **symmetrical**?

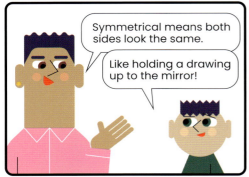

Symmetrical means both sides look the same.

Like holding a drawing up to the mirror!

First, let's protect our table. Can you help us with the **tablecloth**, please?

OK!

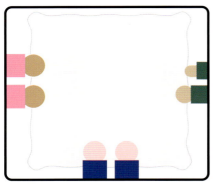

Great teamwork! Now for our **supplies**. Want to help carry them?

Yes please!

What should we do first? Choose our paint colours? Fold the paper? Draw a butterfly?

Choose the **colours!**

Brilliant! You're using **logic.**

What's **logic**?

Logic is where we think carefully about what to do — and what makes sense to do first. Like choosing our colours before we start painting!

Woo!

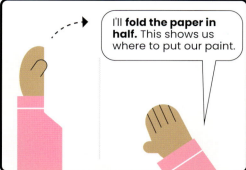

I'll **fold the paper in half.** This shows us where to put our paint.

Can I start now?

Almost! Should I draw a butterfly **outline** first, so you know where to paint?

Yes please! A **big one!**

Good thinking! This will help **guide** your painting.

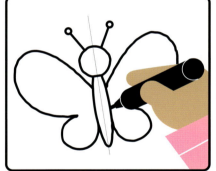

Drawing an outline helps children visualise the final result.

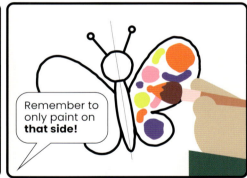

Remember to only paint on **that side!**

FINISHED!

Those colours look amazing together! Ready to **fold it?**

I remember — we **push it down!**

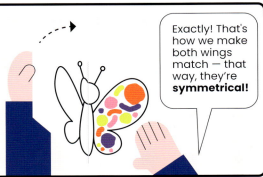

Congratulations!

What a wonderful moment of creativity and logical thinking you've experienced together!

To our Young Butterfly Logician: You made something truly special today! While creating your butterflies, you learnt a great deal about thinking things through carefully. You chose all your colours and followed the steps in order perfectly. You're becoming a brilliant logical thinker — and you did it all while making some lovely art! Every time you make a butterfly, you'll get even better at planning and problem-solving.

To the Adult Butterfly Logician: Today's creative activity has shown how art can be used to teach important computing concepts. Through hands-on experience, your child has practised:

- Logical thinking (planning and thinking ahead)
- Algorithmic thinking (following rule-based instructions)
- Sequencing (putting steps in the right order)

Not only is your child having fun with paint and paper, but they're also building essential foundations for computational thinking; these are the skills that will support their learning when using tools like Scratch later on.

Keep exploring these concepts through creative play, and don't forget to display those beautiful butterflies! Remember, the best learning happens when we're having too much fun to notice we're learning at all.

Taking it further

CREATIVE VARIATIONS

- Draw butterflies of different sizes and wing shapes
- Research real butterflies for design inspiration
- Add decorative details like eyes and antennae
- Use shaped sponges to make different patterns
- Create repeating patterns with shapes and colours
- Experiment with different paint amounts
- Test how paper folding affects the final design

ALGORITHM PRACTICE

- Use simple drawings as instructional prompts
- Practise using sequential language (first, next, then)
- Let the child teach someone else how to make a butterfly

PROBLEM-SOLVING OPPORTUNITIES

- Debug when the paint doesn't transfer well
- Model how to deal with mistakes positively

Remember to introduce extensions gradually after mastering the basics, and always maintain a playful approach to learning.

Activity
Adventures in shopping, logic, and debugging

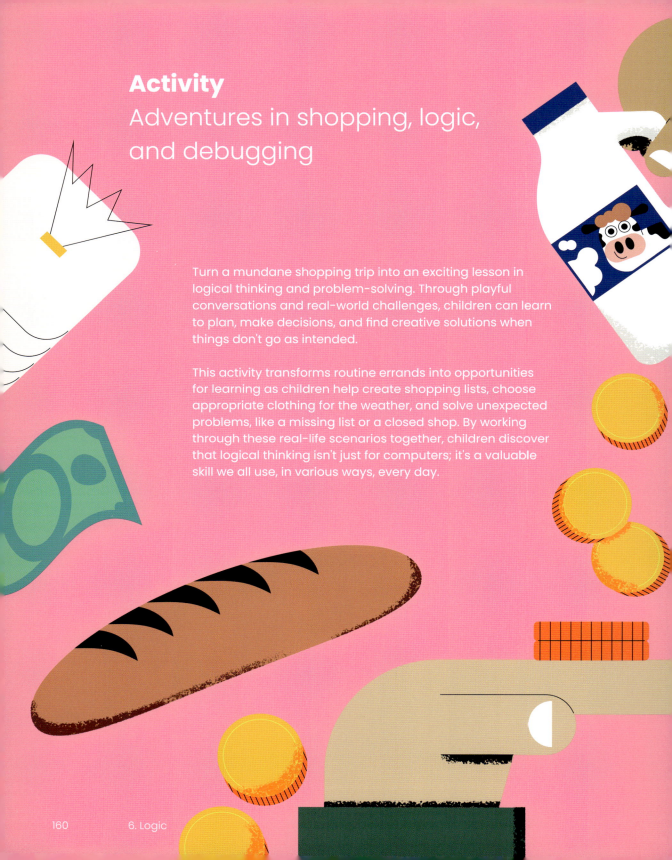

Turn a mundane shopping trip into an exciting lesson in logical thinking and problem-solving. Through playful conversations and real-world challenges, children can learn to plan, make decisions, and find creative solutions when things don't go as intended.

This activity transforms routine errands into opportunities for learning as children help create shopping lists, choose appropriate clothing for the weather, and solve unexpected problems, like a missing list or a closed shop. By working through these real-life scenarios together, children discover that logical thinking isn't just for computers; it's a valuable skill we all use, in various ways, every day.

Materials and prep

TIME NEEDED

- Set-up: 5 minutes
- Activity: 20–60 minutes, depending on your location and mode of transport

REQUIRED

- Shopping list
- Carrier bags
- Money, keys, and other essentials
- Weather-appropriate clothing and footwear

PREPARATION

1. Create a simple shopping list with the child
2. Check the weather forecast and dress accordingly
3. Plan a route to the shops
4. Consider potential challenges to solve
5. Gather any necessary items before leaving the house

BASIC SHOPPING TIPS

- Keep the list short during your first few attempts; start with 2–3 essential items
- Choose familiar products, including items the child can help select

Remember: This activity works best when treated as an adventure, not a chore. Focus on enjoying the journey and the problem-solving opportunities rather than rushing to finish the shopping.

THE LOST SHOPPING LIST

We need to go **shopping for bread, cereal, and milk**. Let's get ready!

OK!

What's the weather like today?

There are lots of **clouds** and **puddles** outside.

And if we walk past any puddles, will you want to splash in them?

Yes! I **love** splashing in puddles!

What should you wear for **puddle splashing?**

MY PUDDLE SUIT!

Why is the puddle suit a good choice?

It keeps me dry when I splash!

Do you remember what happened last time, without it?

I got wet and cold. I didn't like that!

That's right. You've just used **logic** to solve that problem!

Logic helps us learn from past experiences.

What about your feet? Should they get wet?

NO!

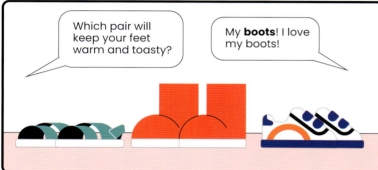

Which pair will keep your feet warm and toasty?

My **boots**! I love my boots!

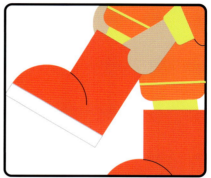

Do you have **the list?**

Yes, it's right here. Ready to go?

Woo-hoo!

AT THE SUPERMARKET

What should we get **first?**

Um... I don't know.

Should we get heavy things first, or light things?

Is this **logic** again?

Congratulations!

What a fantastic journey in logical thinking using everyday adventures!

To our Young Logical Shopper: You've been absolutely brilliant today! Look at all the amazing problem-solving you did — you helped create the shopping list, chose the right clothes for puddle splashing, and worked out what to do when the list went missing. You showed wonderful thinking skills when you remembered the milk by thinking back to breakfast time. That's exactly how all good problem solvers work! Keep using these skills whenever you face a tricky situation; remember how breaking down big problems into smaller ones helps make them easier to solve.

To the Adult Logical Shopper: You've shown how a simple shopping trip can be transformed into a powerful learning experience. Through this everyday activity, your child has practised:

- Logical thinking (choosing appropriate clothing)
- Planning (creating and using lists)
- Decision-making (choosing the shopping order)
- Problem-solving (handling the missing list)
- Memory and recall (remembering items)

Though your child thinks they're just helping with the shopping (and having fun splashing in puddles!), they're actually building essential foundations for logical reasoning and problem-solving. These skills will help them tackle all sorts of challenges as they grow.

Keep finding opportunities for learning in your daily activities, and don't forget to celebrate your successes when solving problems together.

Taking it further

SHOPPING VARIATIONS

- Expand short shopping lists with more items
- Visit multiple shops for different items
- Explore different types of shops (markets, corner shops, clothes shops)
- Create themed shopping trips (birthdays, celebrations)

LOGIC CHALLENGES

- Set up pretend shops at home
- Practise efficient bag packing
- Sort items by type (fresh, frozen, fragile)
- Make substitution decisions when items aren't available
- Work through unexpected problems calmly

TEACHING TIPS

- Let the child write part of the list
- Encourage route planning and navigation
- Use shopping as an opportunity for counting practice
- Make connections to colours and patterns
- Keep activities short and enjoyable
- Make it an adventure rather than a chore
- Be mindful of sensory overload
- Model positive problem-solving behaviour

Remember: The aim is to learn through real-world experiences while still having fun together.

Extension ideas

If your child is enjoying these activities, here are some more ways to explore logical thinking together:

- **Memory cards**
  Match pairs to build memory and association skills
- **List recall games**
  Practise memorising items in order
- **Treasure hunts**
  Follow logical clues ("Look under where we rest at night...")
- **'I spy' with logic**
  Use descriptive clues ("I spy... something that purrs and has whiskers!")
- **Noughts and crosses**
  Practise strategic thinking and planning ahead

Building blocks for coding in Scratch

These logic-based activities develop essential pre-coding skills that help children understand core computer programming concepts. When children practise logical reasoning through their everyday tasks, they begin building stronger foundations for:

- **Problem-solving and deconstruction**
  Breaking down challenges into manageable parts
- **Conditional thinking**
  Understanding 'if this, then that' relationships
- **Sequential reasoning**
  Planning steps in the correct order
- **Debugging**
  Finding and fixing problems systematically

These early experiences with logic make learning to code in Scratch feel more natural and intuitive.

7. Maps, directions, and navigation
Determining your location and planning routes to destinations

Activities

Essential steps

1. Choose a navigation challenge (e.g. following directions, creating routes, reading maps)
2. Show the child how to identify landmarks and use directional language
3. Guide the child to follow and create simple routes
4. Practice finding and fixing navigation errors

Success looks like

- Using directional language correctly
- Following and creating simple routes
- Identifying and using landmarks
- Solving navigation problems

Common challenges

- Too easy → add more landmarks or complex routes
- Too hard → reduce the number of landmarks and simplify directions
- Child loses focus → turn navigation into a treasure hunt or story

Introduction

Why maps, directions, and navigation matter

Understanding maps, directions, and navigation helps us make sense of the world around us. Even in our digital age of satellite navigation and map apps, the ability to recognise landmarks, follow directions, and understand how locations connect remains essential. Starting with simple activities like finding their way around the house, children can quickly progress to going on neighbourhood adventures, until eventually they're ready to tackle more complex navigation challenges.

When children learn to read maps and follow directions, they also develop an understanding of certain computational thinking concepts, including sequencing, algorithms, and debugging. These concepts are key in many areas of life, from simple daily routines and trip planning to learning how to program.

Where we see maps, directions, and navigation

Maps, directions, and navigation are all part of our everyday adventures, whether we're at home, in the local park, or somewhere entirely new. We can spot opportunities to practise these skills everywhere, such as finding our way around a shopping centre, following a trail at the zoo, or creating treasure hunts in the garden; even simple activities like giving directions to the bathroom become chances to teach and learn. The best part is that these concepts can be explored anywhere, from a single room to an entire neighbourhood, and the learning can be as simple or as detailed as you like.

How to explain maps, directions, and navigation to children

When talking about maps, directions, and navigation with children, try these kid-friendly explanations:

> **Adult:** "A map is like a picture that shows us where things are. It has special drawings called landmarks that help us identify where we are based on what's around us — like the big tree, the park, or the shop with the red door."

> **Adult:** "When we're following directions, we need to know our left from our right. Here's a fun way to remember: hold up both hands with your thumbs out. See how your left hand makes an 'L' shape? That's your left side! 'L' stands for 'left'. Let's practise… 'Luh-luh-left and ruh-ruh-right!'"

Adult: *"Let's pretend we're robots walking to the park. Robots can only walk straight ahead or make big turns left and right. Which way should our robot turn to get to the swings? Let's look for landmarks that can help us find our way!"*

Tip: Make it playful! Create simple treasure maps using familiar landmarks in your area.

Activity progress path

Understanding basic directions is the first step in a child's journey towards developing sophisticated navigation and map-reading abilities.

As children progress from learning simple directions to spotting landmarks and creating their own maps, they develop crucial physical, social, and computational thinking skills that can then be extended through additional activities.

CORE ACTIVITY: LOCATING, NAVIGATING, AND MAPPING

- **Basic**
  Learn and use directional language (forward, backward, left, right) to navigate simple spaces
- **Intermediate**
  Identify landmarks, give directions between them, and create simple maps
- **Advanced**
  Plan efficient routes between multiple landmarks and debug incorrect directions

SKILLS DEVELOPMENT

- **Physical**
  Spatial awareness, observation, gross motor skills
- **Social**
  Communication, collaboration, outdoor play/exploration
- **Computational**
  Sequencing, logical reasoning, debugging, algorithms

Troubleshooting tips

When helping children learn about maps, directions, and navigation, you may face some common challenges. Here's how to handle the situation when your child is:

- **Overwhelmed**
  Start with just 2–3 familiar landmarks and simple directions (forward, left, right); add more landmarks gradually as confidence grows.
- **Frustrated**
  Watch for signs of agitation and take movement breaks. Switch to whole-body activities, like pretending to be robots making 90° turns.
- **Confused about left/right**
  Use the L-shape hand trick often. Make it playful by adding silly songs and movements to reinforce their learning.
- **Distracted**
  Clear the workspace and focus on one route at a time. Use their favourite destinations as landmarks to maintain interest.
- **Rushing**
  Turn it into a story or game where each step and turn must be precise. Celebrate when they slow down and get directions right.
- **Showing signs of perfectionism**
  Remind them that even grown-ups sometimes take wrong turns, and that maps help us find our way back when we make mistakes.

Remember: The goal is to help children feel confident exploring different aspects of navigation while keeping the atmosphere playful and supportive.

Exploration awaits
as **Adam** and **Ada**
show you the way!

Activity
Making marble mazes with blocks

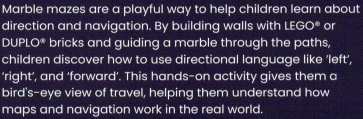

Marble mazes are a playful way to help children learn about direction and navigation. By building walls with LEGO® or DUPLO® bricks and guiding a marble through the paths, children discover how to use directional language like 'left', 'right', and 'forward'. This hands-on activity gives them a bird's-eye view of travel, helping them understand how maps and navigation work in the real world.

As children progress from building physical mazes to drawing them on paper and eventually using real maps, they develop essential spatial awareness skills. This activity naturally introduces concepts like planning routes, following directions, and troubleshooting problems when things don't quite work — all while prioritising fun with marbles and blocks!

Safety note: Adult supervision is required. Marbles pose a choking hazard.

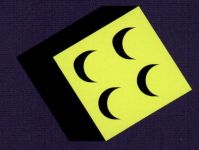

Materials and prep

TIME NEEDED

- Set-up: 5 minutes
- Activity: 10–45 minutes, depending on the child's engagement

REQUIRED

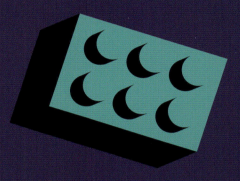

- LEGO or DUPLO bricks in various sizes
- Block baseplate (or cardboard from a cereal box)
- Marbles
- Drinking straw
- Masking tape (if using cardboard base)
- Paper and pencils (optional)

PREPARATION

1. Clear a dedicated workspace
2. Remove any distractions
3. Have drawing materials ready in case your child wants to plan
4. Consider building a simple demonstration maze
5. Check that the marbles are a suitable size for the maze

BASIC MAZE TIPS

- Start with simple paths before adding turns
- Ensure the walls are at least two blocks high
- Make the paths wide enough for the marbles
- Test the paths early to avoid rebuilding later
- Secure loose pieces with tape if needed

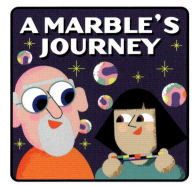

A MARBLE'S JOURNEY

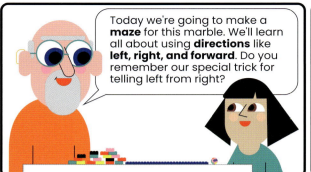

Today we're going to make a **maze** for this marble. We'll learn all about using **directions** like **left, right, and forward**. Do you remember our special trick for telling left from right?

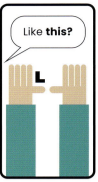

Like **this?**

Perfect! Those hands will help us guide our marble through the **maze.**

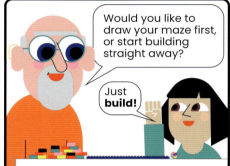

Would you like to draw your maze first, or start building straight away?

Just **build!**

OK! Let's get our blocks ready.

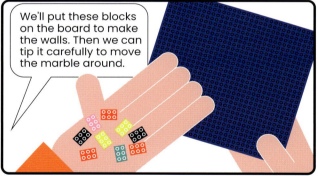

We'll put these blocks on the board to make the walls. Then we can tip it carefully to move the marble around.

Remember, we need the walls to be **tall** so that the marble can't escape!

How tall?

What do you think? Maybe try **two blocks high**...

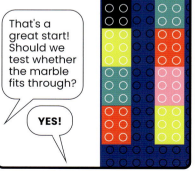

That's a great start! Should we test whether the marble fits through?

YES!

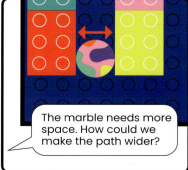

The marble needs more space. How could we make the path wider?

Move the blocks?

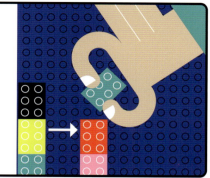

Brilliant debugging! You fixed the problem.

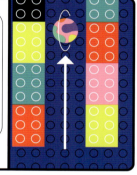

Now we know how wide our paths need to be. It's good we **tested** this early on — imagine if we'd built the whole maze too narrow!

That would be silly!

Where should our marble **start** its journey?

It starts **here**...

...and it needs to end up **here**!

Great! Remember to **leave enough space**, just like we learnt.

I will!

SOME TIME LATER...

Wonderful! Time to **test** our maze! Let's practise those lefts and rights.

Finished!

Let's use our handy left–right reminder. When I put my hands up like this, my **left hand** makes an **L** shape

L for **left**!

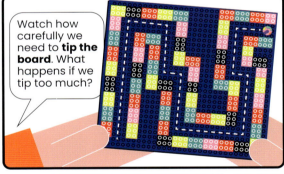

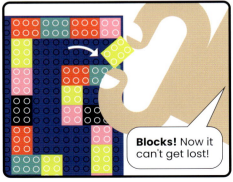

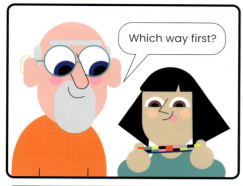

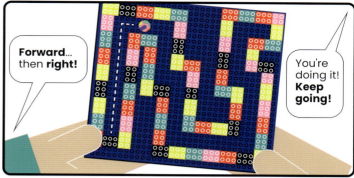

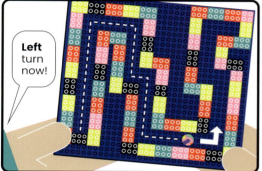

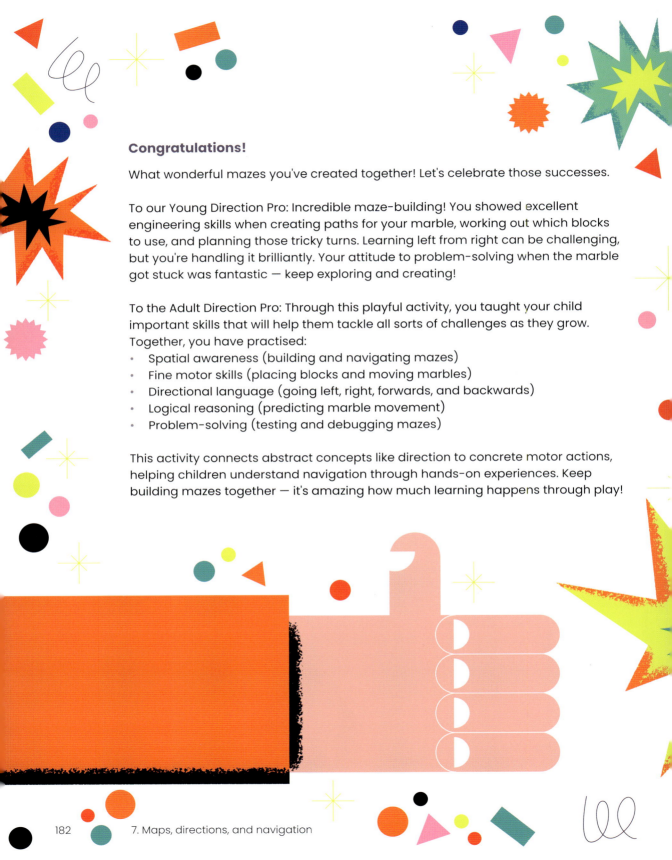

Congratulations!

What wonderful mazes you've created together! Let's celebrate those successes.

To our Young Direction Pro: Incredible maze-building! You showed excellent engineering skills when creating paths for your marble, working out which blocks to use, and planning those tricky turns. Learning left from right can be challenging, but you're handling it brilliantly. Your attitude to problem-solving when the marble got stuck was fantastic — keep exploring and creating!

To the Adult Direction Pro: Through this playful activity, you taught your child important skills that will help them tackle all sorts of challenges as they grow. Together, you have practised:

- Spatial awareness (building and navigating mazes)
- Fine motor skills (placing blocks and moving marbles)
- Directional language (going left, right, forwards, and backwards)
- Logical reasoning (predicting marble movement)
- Problem-solving (testing and debugging mazes)

This activity connects abstract concepts like direction to concrete motor actions, helping children understand navigation through hands-on experiences. Keep building mazes together — it's amazing how much learning happens through play!

Taking it further

BUILDING CHALLENGES

- Create repeating patterns when building the walls (e.g. alternating colours)
- Add intentional dead ends as problem-solving opportunities
- Test different wall heights to see if the marble stays in or is harder to see
- Time different routes through the maze

STORIES AND PLAY

- Make up tales about the marble's journey
- Add themed decorations to create a world
- Guide the marble with sound effects (e.g. "Zoom!" and "Bump!")
- Let the child's imagination shape the building process

TEACHING OPPORTUNITIES

- Track the marble's path with arrows
- Count turns made and blocks/colours used
- Make predictions about the marble's movements
- Exchange mazes and solve each other's puzzles
- Follow the child's lead with new ideas
- Switch roles — let the child create 'bugs' for you to find

Activity
Map-making with landmarks

Time to explore how we use directions in the real world! In this activity, we'll create a simple map using places our children see often. Think about landmarks they know well: the library, their nursery or childminder's house, the local shop, that house with the friendly cat in the window, or the park with their favourite swing. These familiar spots make perfect reference points when learning about maps and directions.

This activity builds on basic direction skills, helping children see how 'left', 'right', and 'forward' connect to real places they know and love. We'll use pictures of these landmarks to practise finding our way between them.

Materials and prep

TIME NEEDED

- Set-up: 5–10 minutes
- Activity: 15–45 minutes, depending on the child's engagement

REQUIRED

- Plastic cups, beakers, or blocks
- Plain paper (2–3 sheets)
- Pens or pencils
- Child-friendly scissors
- Blu Tack or masking tape
- Small figure with a face (doll or LEGO figure)
- Small toys representing local landmarks (optional)
- Glue stick to make permanent maps (optional)
- Clear, flat surface to work on

PREPARATION

1. Clear the workspace of distractions
2. Either:
   a. Pre-select some familiar landmarks, or
   b. Let the child choose their favourites
3. Draw simple outlines of the chosen landmarks
4. Cut out the landmarks as squares
5. Set aside an envelope to store the pictures for future use

Top tips: Keep the drawings simple — basic outlines work perfectly. Store the cut-outs for a quick on-the-go activity and use them when out and about!

THE LANDMARK ADVENTURE

Can you see any places you recognise from our area? We call these **landmarks**.

The house with the cat, the doctors', the train station, the big shop, the cake shop, and the library!

You know so many places!

Could you turn the cups **upside down?** We're going to stick the landmarks to them.

OK!

Using cups as stands makes the landmarks easier to see and move around.

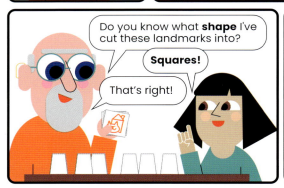

Do you know what **shape** I've cut these landmarks into?

Squares!

That's right!

Can you put some Blu Tack on these, please? Then we'll stick them to the cups.

I'll put these two here. Where would you like to put the others?

Hmm...

INTRODUCING **FINGER WALKING**

Are your walking fingers ready? Show me!

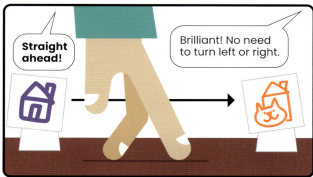

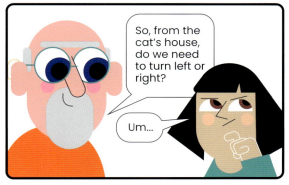

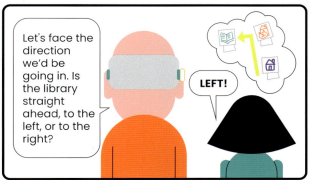

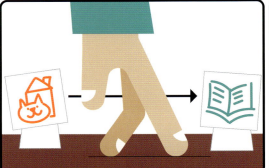

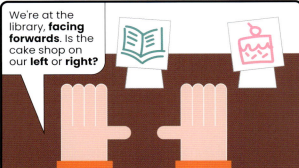

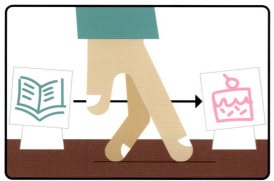

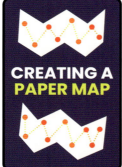

Congratulations!

What a fantastic journey of discovery using landmarks and directions!

To our Young Map-Maker: Brilliant work developing your navigation skills! You've learnt how to use landmarks to find your way from place to place, just like a computer uses a prompt to follow a series of instructions. When finger walking, you showed excellent understanding of directions, and you're becoming an expert at working out left from right. These skills will help you explore the real world and solve all sorts of puzzles along the way. Keep looking for landmarks wherever you go!

To the Adult Map-Maker: Through this playful exploration of map-based navigation, your child has practised:
- Directional language and spatial awareness
- Sequencing and algorithmic thinking
- Problem-solving and debugging
- Decision-making and planning
- Focus and attention to detail
- Fine motor skills

These foundational skills support their development in maths, geography, and computational thinking. By making navigation fun and interactive, you've helped your child build confidence in tackling direction-based challenges. Keep exploring these concepts in your everyday activities — whether you're walking to school or finding toys in different rooms.

Remember: The best learning happens through play and discovery. Keep making maps, finding landmarks, and enjoying the adventure together!

Taking it further

SIMPLE EXTENSIONS

- Create a world you can navigate using toys and blocks
- Find the shortest paths between different landmarks
- Move the landmarks around to create new routes
- Let the child create their own landmarks
- Act out walking using toy figures with moveable limbs
- Practise following and giving directions while walking between rooms

TEACHING TIPS

- Practise the finger-walking position first
- Start with 2–3 landmarks, adding complexity gradually
- Mix familiar landmarks with new ones
- Encourage both verbal and quiet thinking
- Keep the focus on having fun, not on testing accuracy

EXTENSION IDEAS

- Create simple algorithms (go forward, turn left, etc.)
- Let the child create routes for others to follow
- Make deliberate mistakes to encourage debugging

Activity
Debugging maps

Welcome to a fun activity involving planning routes and solving navigation puzzles! Using our familiar landmark props, we'll create and debug routes through different storytelling and problem-solving scenarios.

This activity introduces debugging — the process of finding and fixing problems — in a playful way. In this example, we'll use a story about shopping for bread and frozen peas to help children work out the best sequence to visit places in. They'll need to think carefully about the order: after all, we don't want melted peas!

Using two home landmarks can help us visualise how routes start and end at the same place. Laying out the landmarks in a line shows children that navigating is all about doing things in sequence — in the same way a computer program follows steps in order.

Remember: The goal isn't to achieve perfection but to build confidence in solving problems and explaining solutions. Through gentle questioning, we'll help children discover the answers for themselves.

Materials and prep

TIME NEEDED

- Set-up: 5 minutes
- Activity: 15–45 minutes, depending on the child's engagement

REQUIRED

- Landmarks from the previous activity
- Extra copy of the home landmark
- Plastic cups or blocks
- Plain paper (2–3 sheets)
- Pens or pencils
- Child-friendly scissors
- Blu Tack or masking tape
- Small figure with a face (doll or LEGO® figure)
- Clear, flat surface to work on

PREPARATION

1. Clear the workspace of distractions
2. Draw or trace your landmarks (make two for home)
3. Cut out the landmarks as squares
4. Add Blu Tack to prevent slipping
5. Arrange the landmarks in a top-to-bottom sequence

Top tip: Use upside-down cups to raise the landmarks. This helps prevent the pieces from being brushed off the table during finger-walking practice.

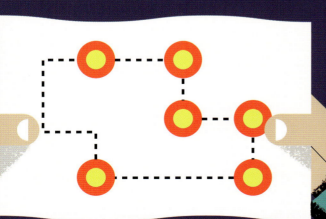

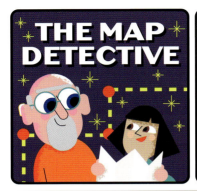

THE MAP DETECTIVE

Remember how we made a **map** that takes us from our house to all our favourite **landmarks?** You found them all and drew the perfect **route line!**

I love the house with the cat in the window!

Now we'll use the same method to think about **sequencing** and **debugging.** I'll tell a story about our landmarks, and you'll help me work out the **right order** to go in. Listening ears ready?

We need to buy **bread** and **frozen peas**, return a few **library books**, and make a quick stop at the **cake shop!** Where do we **start?**

We start at **home!**

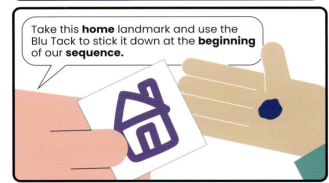

Take this **home** landmark and use the Blu Tack to stick it down at the **beginning** of our **sequence.**

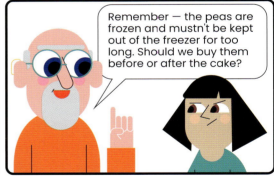

Remember — the peas are frozen and mustn't be kept out of the freezer for too long. Should we buy them before or after the cake?

After! We don't want melty peas.

No one wants melty peas! So, where on our route should the **supermarket** go?

At the **end.**

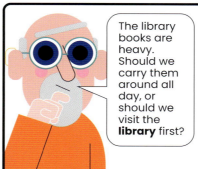

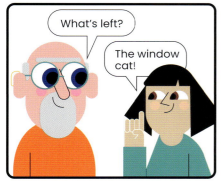

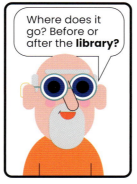

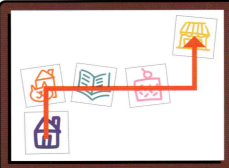

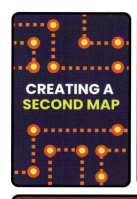

CREATING A SECOND MAP

Let's make a **new map** using these **landmarks.** First, we have to arrange them like these cups on the table.

Can I have the **Blu Tack?**

Of course! You're doing brilliantly.

Now draw some lines between the **landmarks** in our sequence.

Home, cat, library, cake, shop, home!

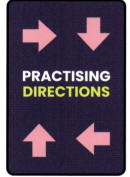

PRACTISING DIRECTIONS

Walking fingers ready?

Ready!

How do we get from **home** to the **cat's house?**

Straight ahead!

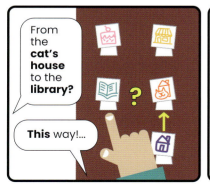

From the **cat's house** to the **library?**

This way!...

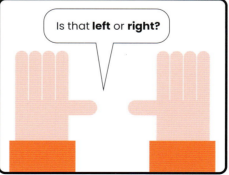

Is that **left** or **right?**

LEFT!

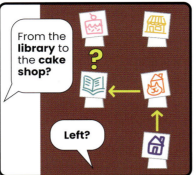

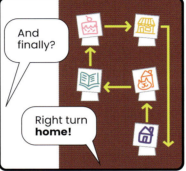

On our journey, we learnt how to plan logical routes, use directions, fix space problems, make clear maps, and debug problems effectively.

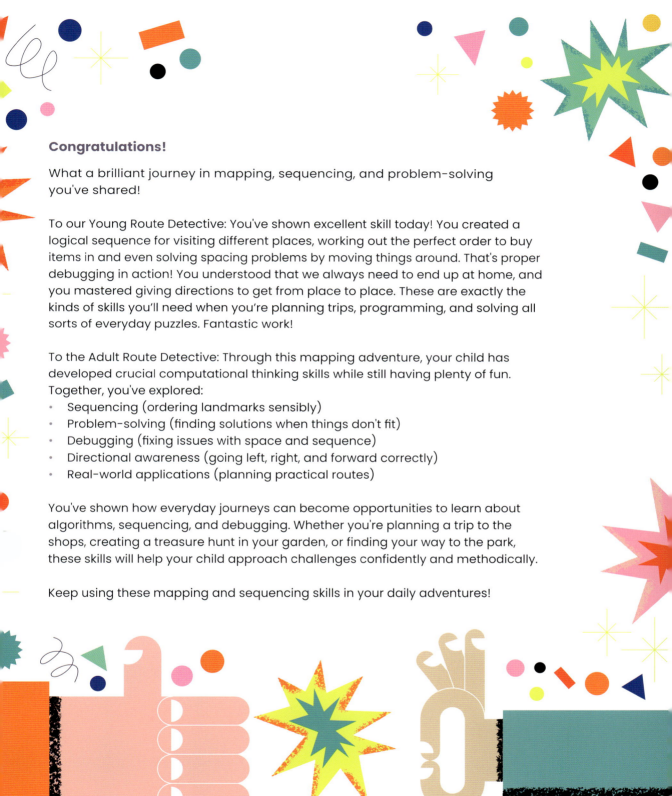

Congratulations!

What a brilliant journey in mapping, sequencing, and problem-solving you've shared!

To our Young Route Detective: You've shown excellent skill today! You created a logical sequence for visiting different places, working out the perfect order to buy items in and even solving spacing problems by moving things around. That's proper debugging in action! You understood that we always need to end up at home, and you mastered giving directions to get from place to place. These are exactly the kinds of skills you'll need when you're planning trips, programming, and solving all sorts of everyday puzzles. Fantastic work!

To the Adult Route Detective: Through this mapping adventure, your child has developed crucial computational thinking skills while still having plenty of fun. Together, you've explored:

- Sequencing (ordering landmarks sensibly)
- Problem-solving (finding solutions when things don't fit)
- Debugging (fixing issues with space and sequence)
- Directional awareness (going left, right, and forward correctly)
- Real-world applications (planning practical routes)

You've shown how everyday journeys can become opportunities to learn about algorithms, sequencing, and debugging. Whether you're planning a trip to the shops, creating a treasure hunt in your garden, or finding your way to the park, these skills will help your child approach challenges confidently and methodically.

Keep using these mapping and sequencing skills in your daily adventures!

Taking it further

ROUTE VARIATIONS

1. Create routes with different starting points
2. Plan routes based on time constraints (quickest route, leisurely route)
3. Plan routes based on different priorities (important tasks first, fun activities last)
4. Add new landmarks to increase complexity

MAPPING EXTENSIONS

- Add street names and road features
- Include distance markers between the landmarks
- Design maps for different purposes (tourist map, delivery route)

TEACHING TIPS

- Let the child take control of route planning
- Use directional vocabulary consistently (left, right, forwards, backwards)
- Make debugging a natural part of the planning process

Extension ideas

If your child is enjoying themselves, then carry on! Here are some engaging ways to build on their learning:

GRID NAVIGATION

1. Create a grid on the floor using paper squares
2. Place the landmarks in different squares
3. Use robot moves: go straight square by square, only turning at right angles

STORY-BASED ROUTES

- Add a twist to the journey: say you're meeting friends at a landmark at 3:00 PM and challenge the child to figure out when to leave
- Create different routes for different weather conditions
- Plan routes around special occasions or events

REAL-WORLD APPLICATIONS

- Use maps at local attractions (zoos, museums, parks)
- Create treasure hunt routes at home
- Design landmark-based walking routes in your neighbourhood

Building blocks for coding in Scratch

When children learn to follow directions, spot landmarks, and sequence steps, they also develop some essential pre-coding skills. These include:
- Understanding sequential instructions
- Planning routes and movement sequences
- Navigating using directional commands
- Debugging incorrect directions
- Using picture-based instructions
- Creating visual algorithms
- Thinking logically

Practising navigation early helps make the transition to Scratch programming more natural and intuitive, while also building real-world problem-solving abilities that extend far beyond coding.

8. Conclusion
Collaboration, communication, inclusivity, and representation

Throughout this book, we've explored the importance of nurturing computational thinking in young children through screen-free, play-based activities. These activities are designed to lay the foundations for future coding skills and, perhaps more importantly, to develop fundamental ways of thinking that will help our children thrive, regardless of the path they take.

The learning experiences presented in each chapter are built on four further essential themes, all of which naturally occur during the activities: collaboration, communication, inclusivity, and representation. The beauty is that children develop these skills almost by osmosis — they're learning while simply having fun. In today's world, where kids are growing up alongside AI and other technologies in ways we never imagined, these particular social building blocks matter more than ever.

While technology can be a brilliant enabler, the greatest progress usually happens when humans work together — when everyone's views are heard and their experiences respected. I've seen this in action with children as young as three; it's truly magical watching them work together, and even better seeing things click for them once they've discussed the activities with one another.

Let's explore how each of these themes shapes our children's learning journey.

Core themes

Collaboration

Working together is fundamental to how we progress as a society. I've witnessed first-hand how collaboration naturally develops in children; it can be as simple as one saying to another, "Can you help me with this? You're really good at it!" or, "I can show you how to do that, if you'd like." When children learn to work together from an early age, they not only develop teamwork skills but also an ability to recognise and champion both their own strengths and the strengths of others. This makes them more adept at solving problems and more empathetic as learners and collaborators — qualities that are becoming increasingly more valuable as technology continues to reshape how we work and learn together.

Communication

Communication goes far beyond just speaking — it encompasses all the ways we exchange information, ideas, and feelings. Children need strong verbal and written articulation skills to express their thoughts and intentions effectively, and these skills are developed through early experiences in collaborating with others. When taking part in computational thinking activities, children learn to express their ideas and thought processes logically and articulately, building their confidence in asking questions and seeking feedback more broadly.

Inclusivity

Creating an inclusive environment means adapting spaces, activities, and opportunities to ensure that everyone can participate fully. We can teach children to think about different perspectives by encouraging them to ask questions like, "Could someone using a wheelchair do this easily?", "Would this make sense to someone who is blind?", or "How might someone who needs extra time understand these instructions?" This approach helps children recognise that the best solutions are those that work for all people, teaching them to take into account the diverse ways we move, see, think, and learn.

Representation

Representation works in two vital ways: it enables children to express themselves authentically and advocate for their needs, and it also addresses the imbalance in STEAM fields. The phrase "you can't be what you can't see" emphasises the idea that children need real-world examples and role models who share their culture, background, or lived experience to help them envision their potential futures. When children only see one type of person in scientific or technical roles (or any role, for that matter), they may unconsciously absorb the message that these fields aren't for people like them.

This is why it's crucial that we showcase the diverse talent working in technology, scientific research, engineering, and inventing. There are already plenty of incredible examples — from disability rights activist Judith Heumann's work in accessible technology and Mae Jemison's groundbreaking contributions to space exploration, to the Indigenous scientists combining traditional knowledge with modern research, and the work done by Anne-Marie Imafidon (co-founder of Stemettes) and Alexandra Knight (founder and CEO of STEMAZING) to inspire the next generation of innovators. When children see such diversity, they're more likely to believe in their own capabilities and feel confident pursuing similar paths.

Looking forward

As your children become more confident using these foundational skills, you may want to start introducing screens and other digital tools. Always use screens with clear learning goals in mind; while coding platforms like Scratch build very effectively on these concepts, they work best when combined with physical, real-world activities. Screens should supplement, rather than replace, activities like the ones in this book.

I take comfort in knowing that whether our children end up as artists, engineers, teachers, or something we haven't even heard of yet, the core skills they're building now — figuring things out, thinking deeply, working with others, and coming up with new ideas — will help them find their way.

Most importantly, they'll carry forward their understanding of how to work with others, communicate effectively, include diverse perspectives, and represent different voices in their work. These social skills, combined with the computational thinking abilities developed here, will help them navigate whatever the future holds.

Final thoughts

I hope these ideas have sparked your enthusiasm and creativity rather than overwhelmed you. Remember that every parent's journey is different. There will be times when you can plan complex learning activities and others when meeting basic needs is all you can manage. Both are perfectly fine. What matters is creating a space where children can ask questions and learn as they play.

Embrace these precious moments of curiosity and growth. Here's to many years of play and exploration with your children!

We'd love to hear about your thoughts and experiences with *Unplugged Tots*; drop us an email or follow the link below. Thanks!

hello@unpluggedtots.com

tinyurl.com/UnpluggedTots